Core Values

PATIENCE

Rebekah Robinson
Anne Hamilton

BECKON CREATIVE
PUBLISHING

Core Values: Patience
Rebekah Robinson & Anne Hamilton
First published in Australia by Beckon Creative © 2025
www.beckoncreative.biz

ISBN 978-0-6456090-3-5

Cover & interior design by Beckon Creative

Cover photograph: Masjid Pogung Dalangan | Unsplash
Photographic & watercolour art: KoelschArtLab, InstantClipArtOasis,
  GraphicshackStore, PatternPalette, Dreamflare Studios | Etsy;
  Daria Ustiugova | © 123RF; Zahra Makes | Creative Market;
  Ontheroad, Kevin Carden | Lightstock;
  Mehtap Aybastı, DesignedByAndreaD, Vertex | Creative Fabrica;
  Beckon Creative; engin akyurt | Unsplash.
  Page 21 includes art from other books in this series, listed therein.
Map base: FrankRamspott, Silvio Kaiser | iStock
Icons and diagrams: Beckon Creative

 A catalogue record for this book is available from the National Library of Australia

The authors assert the moral right to be identified as the authors of this work.
Australian spelling and grammar are used throughout this book.

Except where indicated, Scripture quotations are taken from the Holy
Bible, New International Version®, NIV®. Copyright © 1973, 1978, 1984,
2011 by Biblica, Inc.™ Used by permission of Zondervan. All rights reserved
worldwide. www.zondervan.com The "NIV" and "New International Version"
are trademarks registered in the United States Patent and Trademark Office
by Biblica, Inc.™.

The fruit of the Spirit is love, joy, peace, forbearance, kindness, goodness, faithfulness, gentleness and self-control.

Galatians 5:22–23

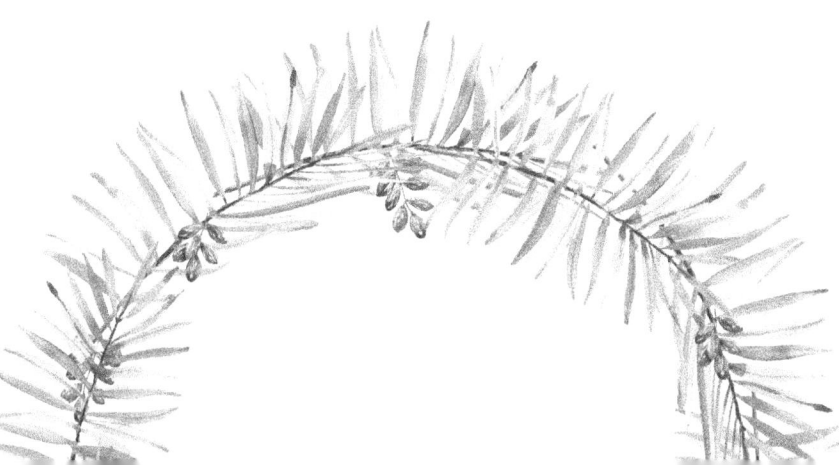

Other Works by Anne Hamilton

STRATEGIES FOR THE THRESHOLD series

Dealing with Python: Spirit of Constriction (with *Arpana Dev Sangamithra*)
Dealing with Ziz: Spirit of Forgetting
Name Covenant: Invitation to Friendship
Hidden in the Cleft: True and False Refuge
Dealing with Leviathan: Spirit of Retaliation
Dealing with Resheph: Spirit of Trouble (with *Irenie Senior*)
Dealing with Azazel: Spirit of Rejection
Dealing with Belial: Spirit of Abuse and Armies (with *Janice Speirs*)
Dealing with Kronos: Spirit of Time and Abuse (with *Janice Speirs*)
Dealing with Lilith: Spirit of Dispossession
Dealing with Rachab: Spirit of Wasting

DEVOTIONAL THEOLOGY series

God's Poetry: The Identity & Destiny Encoded in Your Name
God's Panoply: The Armour of God & the Kiss of Heaven
God's Pageantry: The Threshold Guardians & the Covenant Defender
God's Pottery: The Sea of Names & the Pierced Inheritance
God's Priority: World-Mending & Generational Testing
More Precious than Pearls (with *Natalie Tensen*)
As Resplendent as Rubies (with *Natalie Tensen*)
As Exceptional as Sapphires (with *Donna Ho*)
Spiritual Legal Rights (with *Janice Sergison*)
The Elijah Tapestry
The Summoning of Time
The Lustral Waters

JESUS AND THE HEALING OF HISTORY series

Like Wildflowers, Suddenly
Bent World, Bright Wings
Silk Shadows, Rings of Gold
Where His Feet Pass
The Singing Silence
In the Meshes of the Net
Interpreted by Love

The DNA of God Series

Core Values: Love

Core Values: Joy

Core Values: Peace

Core Values: Patience

Core Values: Kindness, Goodness, Faith

Core Values: Gentleness

Core Values: Self-Control

Core Values: Walking By the Spirit

Grace Drops with Anne podcast:
https://gracedropswithanne.com

Other Works by Rebekah Robinson

Someone to Look Up To: A Lay View of Leadership
(with **Study Notebook** companion)

Day in the Sun (music CD)

Faith Life Art blog: https://beckrblog.wordpress.com

Acknowledgments

Rebekah:

THANK YOU TO THE EVER-PATIENT Trinity. What a blessing it is to be allowed in Your life! Thank You for inviting me into Your heart!

Thank you to my husband Chris and our adult children Daniel & Emma; to our parents, Trevor & Kathryn (Kay) Weavers and Heather Robinson; and to our beloved extended family.

Thank you to Anne Hamilton, who's always brilliant and faithful.

Thank you to all the many friends and leaders in my life, across many decades and three countries, who have been so patient with me on my journey.

The best of the thoughts in these pages are the Lord's; any dodgy bits are all me. It turns out, there's grace for that; but talk it all over with the Lord. The last thing I want is to ever lead anyone astray. Grace and peace to you, and please be patient with me!

Anne:

THANK YOU to Gary, Gary, Ingrid, Judy, Jill, Amybeth, Soo, Tobias, Meaghan, Cathy, Kevin, Jess.

Setting the Scene	10
The Need for Fruit	18
Patience	24
The Patience of God	52
By Their Fruit	89
From the Seed of Hope	106
Prayer: Places to Start	110
Aligning Three Modern Versions	112
References, Symbols and Notes	122

Fruit

- Greek: karpos
- Aramaic: eb
- Hebrew: priy
- NIV: Fruit
- KJV: fruit
- DRB: fruit
- Latin: fructus

fruit, bough, reward;

fruit (as plucked);

qualities of the heart

Setting the Scene

THE CHURCH OF JESUS CHRIST has many faces shown to the world. Sometimes, these 'faces' look askance at one another. My own denomination doesn't think of itself as 'the only true church,' but it can tend to see itself as 'the most enlightened branch'. It does, however, come under criticism from others over one key issue: we seem to be more enamoured with the *gifts* of the Holy Spirit than we are with His *fruit*.

Though it's been a long time since I've heard any focused teaching on the gifts, our siblings have got a point. When you're sure you're the 'bee's knees' and you're producing evidence of the Spirit's presence, what could be amiss? Is not this evident proof of His endorsement?

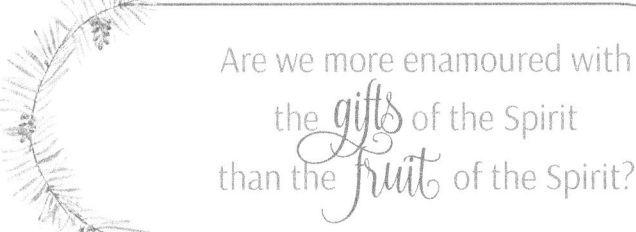

Are we more enamoured with the *gifts* of the Spirit than the *fruit* of the Spirit?

When we look at such 'endorsements' in the Bible, what we see – time and again – is an eclectic list of people with chequered motives, inconsistent devotion, confusion, doubt and poverty, each bringing their mess before the Lord. The kings, priests, apostles and heroes are no exceptions: not all capes wear heroes. It's hard to spot the difference between someone whose ministry is succeeding because they're 'doing it right' and someone whose ministry is succeeding through the immense grace of God, despite them 'doing it wrong'.

And what does God do with such ambiguity? He gives it to us straight. And then He has mercy, and *helps* – as we see in the episode at the 'Gates of Hell' (Matthew 17).

> The fruit of your *ministry*
> ≠
> the fruit of your *life*.

In the end, the fruit of our ministry is a separate thing from the fruit of our lives. The one is the outflow of the fact that the gifts and callings of God are irrevocable (Romans 11:29) and the other is the slow transformation back toward the perfect image of Christ, as we are changed from glory to glory (2 Corinthians 3:18). When Jesus talked in John 15:16 about *'fruit that remains,'* it's likely He was speaking of the fruit of their lives. You can 'do the work' while remaining largely untouched yourself by the presence of God, but the reverse is not true. No amount of good works will conform you into the image of Christ, because that is the role of the Holy Spirit. Apart from the Lord, we can do nothing about our sin-tendency. We can employ behavioural modification; we can adopt scaffolding; we

can train ourselves. But it will only take a particular kind of pressure – the enemy knows this – to bring all of our selfishness right back to the surface. Even when we are fully surrendered to the Lord, this is true. I've wrestled with this: what, then, is the difference beween a 'good pagan' and a 'rotten Christian'?

There is the issue of *ownership*. We are translated from the kingdom of darkness to the kingdom of light; our citizenship has been ratified despite our shortcomings. We are new creations, *'born again, not of perishable seed, but of imperishable, through the living and enduring word of God'* (1 Peter 1:23 NIV). But like all babies, toddlers, children, teens, adults … we must grow into the fullness of His DNA. And that is where walking hand-in-hand with the Spirit comes in. That is what it means to walk humbly with our God: to live with the realisation that we are one slip away, at all times, from deserving the justice He enacts and needing the mercy He delights to show. Becoming born-anew is not a graduation – *well done, bye bye, see you later*. It is an apprenticeship, in the careful company of the Master.

We don't like the straight-talk of Jesus. We prefer the more hippie-like of His traits: *'Let the little children come to Me.'* But if we take out all the frankness of His approach, we are left with a sugar-daddy who will give us anything we want, without consequences or even a pulling-up. But this is not the *real* Jesus. The mercy of God does not exist in a vacuum. It sits next to His justice and His truth.

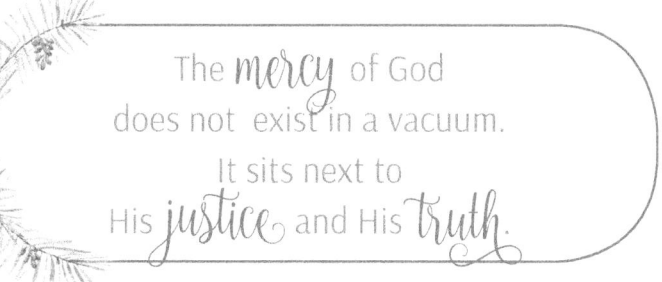

The mercy of God does not exist in a vacuum. It sits next to His justice and His truth.

Forgiveness without correction would be unjust: it would leave us floundering in our mistakes and chasing dead ends. And God the Son, secure in who He is and operating out of a nature of pure love, is qualified to bring it. In much the same way, His strength sits next to His humility. He is all-wise and all-powerful, but also all-empathising.

Just because the gifts and call of the Lord are given by Him *'without repentance'* does not mean He automatically endorses everything we do, or even what we do with these gifts. Think of Balaam in Numbers 22–24. Here was a man who used his prophetic gifts to sell out to the enemy. And yet God still allowed him to keep them, right up until he was slain in Joshua 13 for actual divination. Peter, Jude and Jesus (in Revelation) make him a byword and aren't shy about the kind of guy he was.

The presence of spiritual gifts does not supersede the injunction to do justly, love mercy and walk humbly with our God. It does not exempt us from allowing the Holy Spirit not only to anoint us, but to *amend* us. Invite Him to meddle! By our *fruit* will people know us — not by our manifestations. Operating one of the gifts of the Holy Spirit can be done in a single instant, a moment in time. It is in some senses a 'flash in the pan,' albeit a useful and powerful one. Its focus is on those around us. But living out our partnership with Him as He shapes us? This is about us, and it shows up across our lifespan.

There's comfort in that dilation: nobody is expected to be all things loving, joyful, peaceful, patient and so on, right at the get-go. But it is the general shape we are being moulded into. It is the culture of the Kingdom, which overrides all the lesser faces we show the world, as we turn all of them toward Him. There are many actions (and even antics) we can deal out in our Christian walk and tell ourselves that the end (building the Kingdom) justifies the means (behaving poorly in the process of using the King's gifts). So it's useful to ask ourselves: *is this action I'm about to take for the* pan *or the* lifespan*?* Is there genuine soul-change backing up the temporary performance I'm giving? Am I working for the long haul, or just for an hour's success? Am I pleasing God with my faith in His transformative power, as well as with my deeds? In other words ... am I seeking to *per*form rather than to *trans*form?

> Are we seeking to *per*form or to *trans*form?

In Jesus's last homily before Golgotha, known as the John 13–17 *Farewell Discourse*, He speaks of sending the Holy Spirit to take His place in the disciples' midst. In fact, over dinner and the walk after, He brings up a number of things which we can now identify as belonging to the fruit of the Spirit. (Fruit, *karpos*, is a singular noun: one fruit, not many fruits. This makes Galatians 5:22–23 less of a *list* and more of an *overall picture*.)

Jesus expresses His love in humility (**gentleness**) as He washes the disciples' feet. In **kindness**, He gives them a heads-up that He is not leaving them in the lurch. Jesus tells the disciples that they must **love** one another just as He has loved them. He prays that His **joy** may be in them, and may be complete. He says He is leaving His **peace** with them. He doesn't use the word 'patience,' but He does let them know that there will be a **wait** before they see Him again *'in a little while,'* and also a wait for the Holy Spirit to be given. He tells them as a group to ask the Father in His name for what they need: **faith**. And then He demonstrates **self-control** under the ultimate test conditions, by continuing to cleave to exactly what the Father has asked of Him.

Since we can see these traits in the life and character of Jesus, as well as observing His expectation that they will be accessible with the presence of the Holy Spirit, we could say that they are part of God's 'DNA'. If they were not part of Him, He could not be producing them in us. Humanity was created in the image and likeness of God. Our decision to go our own way marred that creation – but it was reset by the sacrifice and resurrection of Jesus. We can now reflect His nature once more.

> The fruit **of** the Spirit
> can only be produced **by** God's Holy Spirit.
> Fruit is produced in accordance with
> the DNA of its plant.
> Therefore, the fruit **of the Spirit** embodies
> the DNA of God's heart.

Walk with us as we investigate the patience of the One who was, who is, and who is to come.

The Farewell Discourse NIV

'Love one another. As I have loved you, so you must love one another. By this everyone will know that you are My disciples, if you love one another.' — John 13:34

'I have told you this so that My joy may be in you and that your joy may be complete.' — John 15:11

'Peace I leave with you; My peace I give you.' — John 14:27

'In a little while you will see Me no more, and then after a little while you will see Me.' — John 16:16

'I will not leave you as orphans; I will come to you. Before long, the world will not see Me anymore, but you will see Me. Because I live, you also will live.' — John 14:18-19

'I Am the way and the truth and the life. No one comes to the Father except through Me.' — John 14:6

'And I will do whatever you ask in My name, so that the Father may be glorified in the Son. If you ask Me for anything in My name, I will do it.' — John 14:13-14

'Now that I, your Lord and Teacher, have washed your feet, you also should wash one another's feet.' — John 13:14

'I love the Father and do exactly what My Father has commanded Me.' — John 14:31

'The Advocate, the Holy Spirit, whom the Father will send in My name, will teach you all things and will remind you of everything I have said to you.' — John 14:26

The Need for Fruit

WHAT WOULD YOU RATHER HAVE? The full robust and mature suite of Spirit-Fruit flavours or one of the glorious and stunning Gifts of the Spirit in perfectly developed form?

It's a hypothetical question — and the reality is that we shouldn't have to choose. But, for centuries, Christendom has been out of balance on this issue, emphasising one or the other and promoting a Fruit vs Gifts competition that should never exist. It's easy not to notice the rivalry: in some church settings, the Fruit of the Spirit is so completely ignored, it's invisible, while in other churches, the Gifts of the Spirit need to be left at the door like a rain-soaked umbrella.

Now, obviously, in this series of books we're trying to show that the Fruit is not a set of collective virtues that we outgrow when we leave Sunday School. Nor is it a seed that we plant in the garden of our hearts that can just be left untended to flourish on its own.

The Fruit is vitally important. But why?

Now there are many reasons but, just for the moment, let's focus on those that have to do with the invaders of that garden you want to establish as a paradise in your heart. Life is a battleground and, as believers, our hearts are the warzone where the combat between light and dark, good and evil, is played out on a daily basis. In that garden, there's a fight between fallen spiritual powers and the holy ones of heaven — and its Fruit is significant on several key counts:

1. Identification
2. Weaponry
3. Protection

It's important to be able to identify our allies from our opponents. Giving our enemies access to our hearts and aligning ourselves with them is destructive and self-defeating. All too often we assume that we can spot an ally by their spiritual gifts — by the magnificent accuracy of their prophetic words or by the powerful insights in their teaching or by the mind-blowing level of the healing miracles evident in their ministry. But gifts tell us nothing about a person's faith.

We need to remember two things Jesus said and one thing Paul wrote:

1. *'Not everyone who says to Me, "Lord, Lord," will enter the kingdom of heaven, but only the one who does the will of My Father who is in heaven. Many will say to Me on that day, "Lord, Lord, did we not prophesy in Your name and in Your name drive out demons and in Your name perform many miracles?" Then I will tell them plainly, "I never knew you."'*

   Matthew 7:21–23 NIV

Immediately before this, Jesus speaks of how to distinguish between true believers and false prophets.

2. *'By their fruit you will recognise them.'*

   Matthew 7:20 NIV

Paul explains for us why we can't use the Gifts of the Spirit to discern whether or not someone has allegiance to Christ:

3. *'God's gifts and His call are irrevocable.'*

God does not take back His gifts just because we misuse them. They would not be gifts, if He did. However, the exercise of the Gifts without the Fruit straightaway leads to the implementation of power without love, kindness, goodness or self-control: in other words, tyranny.

Apart from identification, the second reason for the importance of the Fruit is that it's weaponry. Back in the Garden of Eden, fruit was weaponised against humanity, so it should be no surprise that the Fruit of the Spirit is now an incomparable armament cache against our spiritual enemies as they try to influence us (and others) to sabotage our walk with Jesus in our heart-garden. Patience is particularly effective against the spirit of wasting. The wonderful thing about the Fruit-weaponry given us by the Lord is that it doesn't harm us, no matter how close we are to the explosion. A joy bomb won't injure us and a love grenade won't damage us — quite the contrary, in fact. They may set off a cascade of healing.

Third, the Fruit is important because it's protection. There is no law against the Fruit of the Spirit. The enemy has no legal right to challenge us for deploying such weaponry. The elements of the armour of light and the divine armour of God are mainly defensive in nature, but the Fruit is offensive.

It comes from being trained and tested — and even sometimes tempted. How, after all, can we mature patience in our lives unless we find ourselves in situations where we feel we're being induced to give in to impatience, frustration and anger? Not every difficult circumstance in life is a spiritual attack: sometimes it's simply resistance training.

Core Values 21 Patience

HEBREW CONCEPT	GREEK	NIV
Love	Agape	Love
Joy	Chara	Joy
Wellbeing	Eirene	Peace
Forbearance	Makrothymia	Forbearance
	Chrestotes	Kindness
	Agathosyne	Goodness
Lovingkindness		
	Pistis	Faithfulness
Humility	Prautes	Gentleness
Self-control	Egkrateia	Self-control

KJV	VULGATE	ARAMAIC RENDERING
Love	Charity	Love
Joy	Joy	Joy
Peace	Peace	Peace
Longsuffering	Patience	Patience
Gentleness	Benignity	Sweetness
Goodness	Goodness	Goodness
	Longanimity	
	Mildness	
Faith	Faith	Faith
Meekness	Modesty	Humility
Temperance	Continency	Endurance
	Chastity	

Patience

Greek *makrothumia*   Aramaic *saber*   Hebrew *erech apayim*   DRB   KJV *longsuffering*   NIV *forbearance*   Latin *patentia*

Longanimity
DRB

Latin
longanimitas

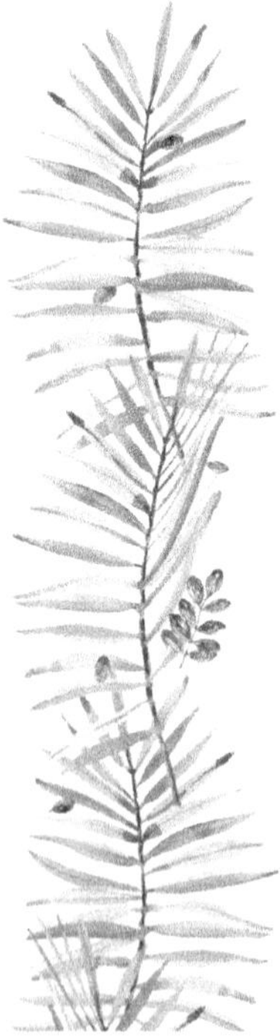

longanimity, fortitude,
patience, waiting, tenacity;
to think and consider

great of sacrifice,
able to endure ill-treatment,
not easily offended, gracious

slow to anger (long-tempered)

one who could avenge himself
but shows restraint

AND NOW WE COME TO THE ONE that sometimes seems like the lemon of the bunch, the fruit-flavour that's a little bitter for some of us: *Patience. Longsuffering. Forbearance. Loooonganimity.* These four words are somewhat distinct, but carry a common thread of *endurance*. Let's have a quick look at each for shades of meaning:

The Picture of Patience

forbearance — to put up with negative circumstances and reserve judgment, punishment or retaliation for another time or another Judge

patience — to wait, confidently and serenely, without becoming irritated or frustrated

longsuffering — to wait steadfastly, while positive change, news, or results take their good sweet time in coming

longanimity — rare tolerance and restraint under provocation or trial

The positive thing about all of these — which I'm going to umbrella under the easy-to-handle word *patience* — is that we are usually talking about a temporary condition:

> ***For now*** *we see through a glass, darkly ...* 1 Corinthians 13:12 KJV
> *After you have suffered **for a little while** ...* 1 Peter 5:10 BSB
> ***As we wait*** *eagerly ...* Romans 8:23 NIV
> *Of this **present** darkness ...* Ephesians 6:12 NAB

My mother, as a young woman, read in Romans 5:3 KJV that *'tribulation worketh patience.'* Accordingly, she opted to avoid any such tribulation by being very, very careful *never* to ask the Lord for patience. Imagine how flabbergasted she was to be told one day on a random altar call: 'Sister ... the Lord wants to give you *patience!*'

Patience does not have to be a word that elicits groans. Patience can be absolutely beautiful, especially when you're on the receiving end of it. Think of a time when you were confused, inept, lethargic, or very ill, and there was someone who was patient with you. Perhaps that's why convalescents are called *patients:* both the sick person and their carers need to let time do its work in that situation. Think of teenagers and their parents ... each slowly learning from the other!

If you've ever seen the movie *The Lake House,* you may remember the wonder in the heroine's voice when, after a two-year stretch apart, the hero finally can and does meet her in person: 'You waited!'

God does ask us to be patient with others, with our lives, with Him, and with His plan. And in true mentor fashion, He sets the example by being patient with us.

In Genesis 6:3 God is recorded as saying, 'My Spirit will not contend [*yadown,* 'shall not strive'] with humans forever, for they are mortal [*basar,* 'flesh']; their days will be a hundred and twenty years.' Since most of us don't even reach 100 these days, that's incredibly generous. It's a written guarantee that His patience will last the entire length of our lives!

Storytime

It's been another long, sweaty day out in Noah's back paddock, toiling away on the giant Thing God's asked him to build. An 'ark', He calls it; *box, basket, casket.* Vessel of the valuable.

Progress is slow going. It takes a lot of timber and pitch to build something so massive; Noah has to buy it piecemeal, which is fine with him, as it takes a long time to actually get the building done anyway. It's an even bet whether he will run out of years before he runs out of money or lumber. Most days, his eventual thought is, 'Man, I need a drink.'

Just last week, he came out in the morning to find that the vandals had been again: splintered bits of wood everywhere, though they left more of the shell intact this time, about 70%. Sometimes they left a huge mess. Sometimes they stacked the shards dangerously, or drove planks into the ground and then broke them off with the sharp ends pointing upwards. It wouldn't be accurate to say that Noah doesn't care; do-overs are frustrating for everyone. Let us say, *he is not deterred.* Build a room, pitch it, fill it with whatever creatures come by (and their fodder). He knows the task God has given him; and knowing it, sticks to it. Every day that he has to fix up what someone broke is another day where he has opportunities to try to persuade more onlookers to join up.

'Hɪᴍ ᴏʀ sᴡɪᴍ' is not a popular message. People don't care that Noah is a nice person. They don't care that he does the right thing, buying supplies over the counter even when it's plain those same supplies were looted from his building site just days ago. They don't seem to notice that his words are motivated by the saving of their lives. All they see is someone who disagrees with their lifestyle choices.

Noah chuckles to himself. Today was Antelope Day, and last month it was Hyrax Day. He just can't wait until Lion Day. Maybe then,

the ill-wishers will let him continue building in peace! They will still walk past and mock him: 'Sky water? Seriously? And ocean geysers? Ooooh, let me go invent the umbrella before a little condensation forms on my brow.' But they might keep their distance once the animals wandering in get a little bigger … if he can keep them from poaching the meaty ones. If he can keep the predators from eating the prey. Luckily, no one last week let the snakes out.

'Do I really have to include cockroaches, Lord?'

Do they have a job to do?

'Well … maybe.'

Then something depends on them. Aren't they amazingly resilient?

'… I guess…'

You know, I designed them to live in one place and do one thing, in limited numbers. Everything changed after Eden. Everything rebelled.

'Point. Um, Lord…'

Mmmm….?

'About the termites.'

If Noah (presumably with a metal box for his termites) is patient because he has a purpose, so is God. God, it seems, is content to move at Noah's speed. And it's slow going, indeed. All the while, society gets more and more violent, more and more audacious, more

and more filthy. It's been years, and I mean *years*, since God asked Noah to begin this task. People are suffering, and insufferable, all this time. Fortunately for Noah, if unfortunately for society, lifespans at this juncture still tend to the centuries. And God seems to want everyone to have a chance. Noah's been preaching the whole time to whomever will listen, but he hasn't had a single convert. So far, it's still a crew of eight people, on a boat built for hundreds. Salvation has been provided for far more people than will ever take up the offer. Many are called — but few are choosing.

This isn't the only example of God's patience in the Old Testament. It took Him 400 years to finally have had enough of the Amorites' abominable child abuse practices, and to wipe them out via Joshua. For each one of us looking at that conquest who thinks, 'That genocide wasn't very nice of God,' there's someone else looking at the previous *lack* of action, and saying the same thing: 'How could He have let that go on so long?'

Romans 3:25 tells us that a righteous God cannot overlook unpunished sin, but He can hold the penalty in abeyance. That's some stretch of patience: to hold contained all the sins committed between the Flood and the Blood. In fact, the same distance forward applies too: otherwise no one born after the time of Christ could ever have their sins forgiven through the Cross, since *all* of those were future sins.

This not only tells us that God is patient, but it tells us very loudly that He's fascinated with us. He *wanted* us to be born and to live and to come into relationship with Him. He found this concept so irresistible and so glorifying that He gave His everything for it.

When we look across the spectrum of the fruit of the Spirit, we can see that some of those core values of God's appear, on first glance, to be responsive (I don't think we can use the word *reactionary* in relation to a God of infinite wisdom and forbearance).

If sin in the created universe did not exist, would God have any need to exercise patience? Would He be called upon to humble Himself into gentleness?

The answer, as you know, is that God does not change; and since His existence predates ours, these are not things He has 'learned' in order to cope with the surprisingly misbehaving creatures He has produced. Quite the reverse. What does a patient Being have to do, in order to get to use their patience? Well ... He could create a range of creatures much stupider than He is. Such creatures need not be *fallen* to be awkward.

If we posit an unfallen Eden – if our forebears had never sinned – would it immediately follow that sorrow would be unknown in the Garden? I think not. A perfect person in a perfect environment is still going to encounter disappointments ('the strawberries are not in season') and they are still going to experience frustrations ('other perfect people have different priorities than I do'). They may bend in acquiescence faster, they may prefer one another more readily, but they are still made of the same emotions we are. Nor could Eden be a place of no bloodshed, because children *will* fall out of trees – even perfect children. Perhaps blood was created red so that punctures could be located with precision.

And so a perfect person in perfect Eden would need to echo the image of God by exercising patience when it is not their turn, or when they cannot immediately get what they want, just as we must.

 Longanimity

The first time I saw this word, I thought it meant *generosity* – perhaps because it looks like it should mean 'long-handed-ness.'

Longanimity is, in fact, long-spirited-ness: an intense, afflicted version of *forbearance*. I stumbled across a beautiful description from *The Modern Catholic Dictionary*:

> *Extraordinary patience under provocation or trial. Also called long suffering. It is one of the fruits* [sic] *of the Holy Spirit. It includes forbearance, which adds to long suffering the implication of restraint in expressing one's feelings or in demanding punishment or one's due. Longanimity suggests toleration, moved by love and the desire for peace, of something painful that deserves to be rejected or opposed.*

It sounds like the Cross, doesn't it? Others add:

- *a disposition to bear injuries patiently*
- *good-natured tolerance of delay or incompetence*
- *rare patience or forbearance*
- *patient endurance of hardship, injuries, or offence.*

For the Church, Eugene Peterson popularised Friedrich Nietzsche's phrase, 'a long obedience in the same direction,' which perfectly sums up patient service in discipleship. It's an amazing and beautiful thing when a lover of God can redeem or 'enlighten' the words of an atheist. And it's even more beautiful, though in a sad and poignant way, to reflect that the Lord had been 'breadcrumbing' that atheist (the originator of the 'God is dead' concept) the whole time – dropping a trail of truth-clues to lead him into the light, had he been receptive.

Regarding this element of 'not demanding what one is owed,' Romans 12:19 and Deuteronomy 32:35 NIV say, collectively,

> *Do not take revenge, my dear friends,*
> *but leave room for God's wrath, for it is written:*
> *It is Mine to avenge; I will repay.* [*says the Lord.*]
> *In due time their foot will slip;*
> *their day of disaster is near*
> *and their doom rushes upon them.*

The implication is that God's perspicacity, thoroughness and timing are far superior to ours. And in addition, He has set up the universe not only with the law of sowing and reaping — *those who live by the sword will die by the sword* — but also with the law of increase. It's tied to the idea of *diminishing returns*. This means that what we start, we escalate. Those who sin against us will find their penalty earning compound interest; but it applies to us, too. If we start a chain reaction of tit-for-tat — however justified it may seem — it will snowball. A fictional example is *Romeo and Juliet:* the long-term cycle of revenge culminates in tragedy all round. Longanimity, on the other hand, calls us to leave things in God's trustworthy hands. Not that it's any kind of sport, but in modern terms, *long*animity is playing the *long* game.

Longanimity is playing the long game on God's team.

Sometimes we see the enemies of truth and love seeming to skate through life and die in relatively untroubled, even prosperous circumstances. Not to be vindictive, but in the same way that we don't get our full reward until we pass, neither do the unrepentant. And yet the highest glory for God is not a sinner duly punished, but a sinner fully redeemed. To turn an enemy into a brother is a far higher victory than to merely see them get the comeuppance they deserve. We, after all, are not getting what we deserve; unmerited grace is our passport to salvation and Heaven. Everything we are getting is coming from the hand of mercy. And God's patience and kindness is what prompts us to ask for it.

If longanimity is to bear up uncomplainingly even under the harshest of conditions or persecution, one might well throw up one's hands and exclaim, 'How on earth does God expect me to do that?!'

The answer is: He doesn't. He knows perfectly well (all too well!) the human nature of needing to vent when things aren't going smoothly. He knows it's not good for us to be alone – that we need each other. But He calls us higher: to make Him our true refuge, the one we run to, the one who can be privy to our deepest hurts and concerns.

So (1) the thought follows, what about all that talk about not grumbling and complaining? Isn't going to God 'for a whinge' complaining? Yet how do we make Him our refuge if we are not allowed to be honest with Him about what we're feeling? Police our emotions better? Suppress them, gaslight ourselves?

Well ... I believe there's a difference between complaining *to* God, complaining *about* God, and complaining to others about others. Perhaps the Israelites under Moses annoyed God because they grumbled amongst themselves, rather than bringing their concerns to Moses and to God. Don't be too hard on them – they were generations past Joseph, who knew God so personally. But don't be too easy on them, either – they'd seen enough spectacular

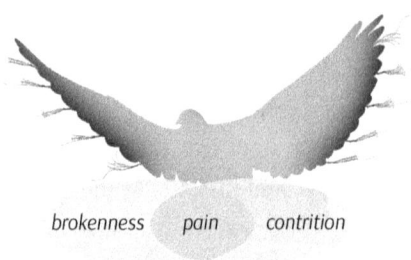

brokenness   pain   contrition

first-hand miracles to be certain God was on their side and in it with them.

God is okay with you bringing Him your true feelings. *'A broken and contrite heart'* – these are overlapping things – *'You will not despise,'* promises Psalm 51:17 BSB. Mainly this verse deals with repentance: God is not disgusted by our abased admission of sin, but welcomes our desire to be righteous and right again with Him, with our trust in His mercy. Heartfelt remorse, humility and faith mean far more to Him than simply giving up a couple of animals, ticking the box, and going on your merry way. But it also shows us, incidentally, that He is not put off by our tears and shatteredness. He is a safe place to bring them. If perchance they are entirely self-serving, He will gradually show us. But He will never not be there for us.

Context should be added here. Philippians 4:4–9 gives us a pattern for unburdening ourselves, and if you'll pardon the audacity, I'll paraphrase:

> *Let the Lord's presence in your life run like a constant underground river of joy through you. Dip often!*
>
> *Let it influence you to treat others with kind humility.*
>
> *Because the Lord is close and intervening and imminent, you don't have to let anxiety have sway. In every situation summon your thankfulness to Him. On that basis, pray – bringing Him your 'asks'. Let His very own transcendent peace safeguard your mental and emotional health, as you remember you belong to Jesus and He's got this.*

Now refocus on things that are wholesome – such as the Lord Himself! – and if you need an example, watch how I do it under trying circumstances. God is all about integrity and wellbeing and wholeness, and I testify that He never bails.

2. The next thought on God's expectation of you is that He does not require you to conjure longanimity by yourself. Far from it.

God is not, at this point in time, filling His rightful role as Judge. That is for later. We are not applying for justification today at a bench where He bangs a gavel and intones, 'Failure to be tortured without whimpering: a hundred hours' community service.'

Instead, He holds out His hand – or the wing of His prayer shawl – and offers to partner with us in managing our pain. The fruit of the Spirit is birthed in us as a seed, slowly growing. This is the New Creation. While it grows, we can borrow from Him His own equanimity, His own wisdom. If we are ever able to get through suffering without buckling, it will only be because He is upholding us with His righteous right hand. Because underneath us are the everlasting arms.

You will not necessarily stop feeling the pain. But you can invest the pain into your relationship with God by running to Him. Strengthen and continually reinforce that bond and partnership with the One who understands, empathises, and ultimately recompenses. Jesus prayed with faith. Reach for the hem of His garment, where you'll find the feathery tassels of His prayer life. He invites you to appropriate it!

Invest your *pain* into your *bond with the Lord*.

Active Waiting, Passive Waiting

The Bible doesn't give us the Hebrew word *savlanut* for 'patience', but we are given one for 'impatience': *laah*. It has connotations of weariness, exhaustion, diffficulty, parchedness, aggravation. It even *sounds* frustrated!

laah — weariness, aggravation

Sometimes translated 'patient' (as in Proverbs 16:32 NIV), *erech 'appayim* is literally 'slow to anger', conflating the two ideas. The Lord is slow to get angry (Exodus 34:6) and this means He doesn't explode with impatience the instant we let Him down. There is no volatility in Him, despite His immense dynamic power and the highest of standards.

erech 'appayim — slow to anger

We are given a beautiful Hebrew word for the passionate patience of 'waiting in expectation': *qavah*. We talked about this in *Core Values: Joy* when we examined the 'serenity' intersection of joy and patience (page 89*ff*). The NIV translates it *'hope in'*, revealing this layer of not just sitting back, but actually employing trust, expectancy and perhaps planning.

There are several Greek terms for 'patience' in the Bible, *hypomenontes* and *makrothumia* being the most prominent. I believe *qavah* to be linked to *hypomenontes*, while others believe it to be more like *makrothumia*. Both appear in 1 Corinthians 13, which says that **love is *makrothymei*** (patient) and that **it hopes and *hypomenei*** (bears) **all things.** All of these words are valuable concepts for us.

Neal D. Presa writes of:

'... *makrothumia*, which combines two word concepts: great distance and passionate fierceness. In short, ferocity

– or, as the King James Version says, "longsuffering". This is the patience of someone who is ferociously wronged, terribly sinned or trespassed against, and who has both the reason, the right, the ability, the opportunity and the power to avenge the wrong, but doesn't do it. That's the patience of the fruit of the Spirit. …

'*Makrothumia* patience is a call not to dream, but to live into what the Spirit of Christ is already doing in us and among us. We just have to pay attention and follow.'

All of these patience-words blur into self-control and meekness: strength held in reserve.

In my personal opinion, *makrothumia* – the fruit-patience – is **passive waiting**, where *hypomeno* and *qavah* are **active waiting**. All one has to do to have *makrothumia* is to stay in control of oneself and trust God for outcomes.

> … He is **patient** with you, not wanting anyone to perish, but everyone to come to repentance.
> 2 Peter 3:9 NIV

makrothumia
patience, longsuffering

The other two terms are more urgent, with a sense of tension. 'Let me at 'em once the moment's ripe.' Or, perhaps, 'I *could* retaliate – but I won't.' Most especially, 'When God is ready, I am too.'

> *I* **waited patiently** *for the* Lord;
> *He turned to me and heard my cry.*
> Psalm 40:1 NIV

qavah
to wait like a taut twined rope

These terms are not in competition, of course, and neither the passion of *makrothumia* nor the oppressedness of *hypomeno* could be accused of indifference. But in practical life, we sometimes have to decide which patience is being called for – active or passive?

Greek

Makrothumia

patience, longsuffering

from *makrós*, 'long' and *thymós*, 'passion, anger': to keep one's temper in calm acceptance and hold oneself in steadfastly, seeing the big picture with self-control, rather than going off half-cocked.

fruit-patience, Galatians 5:22

Hypomeno

to stay behind or under, to await, to endure

from *hupo*, 'under' and *menó*, 'stay, abide, remain': to undergo, bear trials, bear up under, have fortitude, persevere, stay behind; a sense of power held in reserve, like a racehorse at the gate.

patient in affliction, Romans 12:12

Anoché

tolerance, to put up with weakness, forbearance

from *anechó*: to hold up; to hold one's self erect and firm; to sustain, to bear, to bear up under; forbearance, a delaying or suspending of punishment, mercy that holds unnecessary judgment back.

riches of forbearance, Romans 2:4

Apekdechomenoi

to expect eagerly, wait for eagerly, look for

from *apo*, 'away from' and *ekdechomai*, 'welcome': to expect fully. A turning from and a turning to.

wait eagerly, Romans 8:23

Anexikakos

patient, forbearing, enduring evil
from *anexomai* 'to endure or bear with'
and *kakós* 'evil'. To tolerate and not retaliate
when provoked.

**able to teach,
and patient,**
2 Timothy 2:24

Hebrew

Erech 'appayim
slow to anger
from *erek* 'long' and *aph* 'nostril, nose,
face, anger'. It takes a great deal to make the
Lord God snort, huff or breathe fire, darken His face, express
wrath; He never loses His temper, but leads with grace and
compassion. (There was some warhorse-like snorting in
John 11:38 when the death of Lazarus moved Jesus deeply.
In extremis the Lord's emotion shows its strength.)

**slow to
get angry,**
Exodus 34:6

Erech ruach
to take a long time to become angry.
Literally 'long breath, long of spirit'
perhaps implying 'relaxed.'

a patient spirit,
Ecclesiastes 7:8

Qavah
to wait like a taut twined rope
'wait, look for eagerly, hope, expect' in the
sense of twist, stretch, tension, enduring; by extension, to be
entwined, perhaps to be tethered, to plait in anticipation, to
stand alert and committed on duty as a servant on call.

**wait upon
Yahweh,**
Isaiah 40:31

Chakah
to wait, tarry, to long for
with an expectation or hope, patience
and anticipation, fulfillment of a promise.

longs to be gracious,
Isaiah 30:18

Yachal
to wait, hope, expect, be patient
waiting with expectation or hope,
anticipation of the positive or divine

wait for Him,
Lamentations
3:24

intervention. It is a cognate idea to two Greek terms: *elpizo,* 'to hope, expect' (note the *'pis'* of *elpis* is reminiscent of *pistis,* 'faith') and *hupostasis,* 'assurance, confidence'. *Pistis* is the *hypostasis* of things *elpizomenōn* (Hebrews 11:1). It is that which stands up under pressure and that which can be stood upon.

Savlanut
bearing the burden of your suffering
from *sevel,* 'pain, suffering, agony' and
sabal/sebel, 'a porter, load, burden'.
Savlanut does not appear in the Bible, though *sebel* does.

burden removal,
Psalm 81:6

Laah (antonym)
to wear out the patience
weary, become impatient, exhausted,
find difficulty, parched, tired, try the patience.
In today's slang we would say, 'I am *so over* this already!'

try the patience,
Isaiah 7:13

Love is makrothymei (patient) ... *it hopes and* hypomenei (bears) *all things.*

1 Corinthians 13: 4, 7

In the parable of the lump sums (Matthew 25) three trustees are waiting for their master's return. Two of them employ active waiting, using the time to invest and double their money. One of them employs passive waiting, letting the money rot as it is — and is reprimanded severely.

However, in the Garden of Gethsemane it goes the other way. At dinner in Luke 22 the disciples are arming up, though Jesus says, 'Enough!' Peter bides his time until the arrest, when he puts his sword to use, slicing off Malchus's ear. He is then told off for being far too active, when what was called for was to watchfully trust in God's will.

The Latin word *patientem* and the Greek *pathos* (each meaning 'suffering') both play into our word *pathology* ('suffering and disease') — linking the ideas of having to *be* patient when you *are a* patient. The Old French *paciente* (which looks suspiciously related to the peace-words *paix, pax, pacify, pacific* and *pacifist*) meant 'capable

of enduring misfortune without complaint.' In Middle English *anyone* who displayed patience could be labelled 'such a patient.'

Hypomenó is used 'under the pump' in these two verses:

tribulation worketh **patience**	KJV
suffering produces **perseverance**	NIV
trials ... help us develop **endurance**	NLT
affliction perfects **patience**	ABPE

hypomonén
to stay behind or under, to await, to endure

Romans 5:3

Be joyful in hope, **patient** *in affliction, faithful in prayer.*
Romans 12:12 NIV

Makrothumia is also featured in Romans:

chrēstotētos
goodness, kindness

Or do you show contempt for the riches of his **kindness**, **forbearance** *and* **patience**, *not realising that God's kindness is intended to lead you to repentance?*
Romans 2:4 NIV

anochēs
tolerance, to put up with weakness, forbearance

makrothymias
patience, longsuffering

God's patience and kindness have a purpose: our liberation from sin, and our deep personal alliance – covenant – with His heart. It's not a case of laissez-faire ('whatevs'), but a case of setting up the conditions most conducive to draw us to Him. If this sounds manipulative, or too clinically strategic, remember that God is, Himself, *Love*. Any strategy born of love – true, altruistic, sacrificial, putting-the-beloved-first love – comes from fire, not from ice. He engineers His patience towards our repentance because covenant with Him is what will evolve us into the satisfied, glorious lovebeings we were designed to be.

# Waiting For, Upon, and On God

Qavah is living the waiting-life entwined with God and His will. We are enmeshed, if you like: so attuned and wrapped up in Him that His desires become our desires, and He only has to say the word, and we're 'on it.' That's the theory, at least; most of us have a little whinge before we get off the couch and go do what the Lord has told us to do. We might fantasise about the romance of being completely God's, but it takes a while for us to get there in practice. And so He has to wait for us, as well.

Qavah is also about not wearing out your energy before its moment of greatest import. It's for the marathon, not the sprint. Think of the parable of the ten bridesmaids. Five of them let their oil fritter away instead of reserving it (with further reserves) for the proper time. The Bible promises that waiting for God will renew us,

*They that **wait upon** the LORD*
shall renew their strength;
they shall mount up with wings as eagles;
they shall run, and not be weary;
and they shall walk,
and not faint.

Isaiah 40:31
KJV

not deplete us – despite the tension involved. Muscular tension develops strength.

This is a *preparatory* patience, not passive inactivity. It gets itself situated into a position to receive. It doesn't dither. This is the prodigal's father, on the verandah in his Nikes and binoculars. He's not inside watching TV. On our side, this patience hinges on resting in the nearness of a working, good, invested God.

> *Wait patiently for the Lord;*
> *be strong and let your heart take courage.*
> *Qavah el Yahweh!*
>
> Psalm 27:14 BSB, ESV, Hebrew

This idea of living 'on call' is reminiscent, of course, of our service expression 'to wait on someone'. We've heard that expression in everything from sales to royalty. It has the same impetus: it's not about tapping the foot and checking the watch. It's about *ever-ready service*. We 'wait upon God' in the sense of being ready to supply whatever He commands. We wait on Him hand and foot, as handmaidens wielding the sword of the Spirit and foot soldiers standing on the foundations of the peace-gospel. We are vassals to our Suzerain – but *this* King reciprocates that focused attention, lifting us up rather than wearing us down. His Spirit enables us to go the distance with His stamina-giving grace. This cycle of attentive obedience, reward, and gratitude is so beautiful.

We may be asked for a long obedience in the same direction, but God is also giving us a long faithfulness in the reverse direction. Our tension in waiting is surely not more powerful than His.

The word *prodigal* does not mean 'wandering'. It's from the word family of *prodigious*, and in the parable it's used to indicate that the son went completely overboard in spending a lot of money and living wildly. Yet guess where he got his *don't-do-things-by-halves* from? His dad poured out all his integrity, generosity, love, forgiveness and celebration to such an extent that the parable might as well be known as *'The Prodigal Father.'*

Storytime

It's been so long since he left.

I think about him *every day*. Not that I approve of what he did — not ever — but oh, my heart goes out to him. *My son. Where are you? Are you all right? Come home. I don't care about the money. I just want you back.*

I know, broadly speaking, what he's up to. I saw the signs before he went. I know he likes the girls, the drink, the parties, the finer things in life. If he'd asked me, when he was still living at home — if either of my boys had asked me — I would have supplied every need, and a few 'wants' into the bargain. But he never asked. I suspect it's because my young spendthrift knew that the things he wanted, in the amounts he wanted them, would have shamed him to put into words.

You could have cut my heart out with a spoon when he came up with his request. 'I want my inheritance now, while I'm young enough to enjoy it.' Never mind that he's far *too* young for such a precious burden. No. What cut wasn't his desire for a sinful lifestyle; it was his preference for *fortune* over *father*. If he'd said, 'Dad, I wish you were already dead,' it would barely have been a more blatant 'blow you'. All of this affluence I've amassed for my boys; and after all that, after decades of careful management and planning and providence, I'm worth less to him than the ink on my bank statement.

Oh, I could have said no. But I decided a long time ago that I wasn't going to be a puppet-master. You don't garner love with control. If it's not freely given, it's not real. He's of age and he can make his own choices ... even the devastating ones. The ones that rip your guts out and signal disaster.

So why do I still care?

Same reason King David cared, even though his son stole the hearts of his subjects, swiped the harem, assassinated his brother, staged a coup, and rendered his king and father homeless: *He's my son.* I'll always love him. No amount of rebellion, stubbornness, or hair-raising antics will change my emotional investment in his welfare, nor my commitment to him. Children are a heritage from the Lord. They're a gift without recall.

I kept tabs on my boy's whereabouts, right up until he disappeared from public life and the society pages. Now, it's a mystery. Sometimes I imagine him, living it up big somewhere overseas, making a packet and flying high. But I doubt it. He hadn't built any acumen before he left, and I doubt it found him on the party circuit. Sometimes I'm troubled by dreams of him, out of funds and destitute, hungry and dirty. I hope he's not … but he may very well be. He wasn't particularly savvy with people, and never had much aptitude for managing money. That's his brother's forte.

His brother doesn't understand me very well, even after sticking around all these years and working diligently. He's a good lad, but he keeps me at arm's length – to say nothing of his sibling. He thinks we should write the boy off. (As if I could!) He assumes I'm a great deal stingier than I really am, as if the loss of half the assets renders me at all poor or less of an entrepreneur. I'm doing fine, in fact; the passive income from investments has levelled us back up to where we were. If the greedy youngest had waited, he'd have had a far greater nest egg waiting for him, as does his starchy brother.

I keep waiting for the latter to ask me the small things: 'Could I throw a party? Could I this? Could I that?' But he never does. Maybe he thinks it'll tarnish his martyr-image. I'm proud of his work ethic, but I do wish he wouldn't treat me like an employer. I'm his *dad*. I'm here for him – always was, always am, and always will be in the years to come.

So. I wait. One day, I hope and pray my youngest comes home to us. To me. And if and when he does — what will he find?

Scolding? I expect life will ream him out more than enough. Degradation? Humiliation comes to everyone who makes foolish choices; I won't add to it. Relegation? No. He's my son; he'll always be my son. And once that corner is turned, I will shield us both from any loss of dignity. He's a son of my House and I'll proudly help him resume that part.

That's why I'm getting things ready. I've got a thousand head of cattle producing magnificently. Each year the calves get bigger and fatter, and I always keep a few at home on market day. You never know when a celebration may be called for. I dream about it.

In the entrance hall, there's a wardrobe; all the senior staff know it's reserved. There's ten clean sets of good clothes in there, dust-protected in garment bags; I have things checked and updated every year on his birthday. I don't know which season he might return in — if ever. There's one of the family's coded signet-rings, in a locked box. And the finest footwear on the market. It's all waiting.

And so am I. I'm on this verandah every day, binoculars out, drones up, shoes on, heart in my mouth. Can I move quickly, in this business suit? You bet I can. I've been working out; I've made sure of it. Because when I see him — *oh, I miss you so much, just COME HOME, SON!* — I'm gonna **RUN**.

Kindling

Throughout the Bible there are occasions where the writers use the expression, *'The anger of the Lord was kindled ...'* This phraseology is masterful.

I grew up in New Zealand in the 80s, the middle winter months necessitating a daily fire. If you've never seen a fire started with kindling before, this is how it went: you started with scrunched-up newspaper, then you added some small dry sticks on top (the kindling). Finally on went a couple of larger logs. Then you lit the newspaper. In a fireplace, paper burns fast; the kindling catches the flame after a bit, and burns at medium-speed; and eventually the logs get the idea, and burn slowly into embers.

Does the Lord experience anger? Yes, He does. Anger itself is therefore not a sin, for the Lord never sins. He does, however, warn us rather drily in James 1:20 that *human* anger does not produce the righteousness of God. There's a big difference between *righteous anger* and *using anger righteously* – and we are not very good at it.

He, however, shows us something rather beautiful. 'Kindled' is from Hebrew *charah*, 'to be hot, to burn, to be angry, to be kindled, to glow, grow warm, blaze up with rising intensity' – in short, to escalate.

The Lord does not fly off the handle. He does not go from 0 to 100 in 1 second. There's no lashing out without warning. Yes, there are episodes where swift discipline occurs, such as the steadying of the Ark of the Covenant. But there are always warnings.

In that particular case, if David had studied the Torah daily, as was required of a king, he'd have known how the Ark was to be transported – the relevant data having been available for several centuries. It would never have been on a cart in the first place, and it would never have been treated like 'the fancy chest we've been keeping in the garage the last few years.' 2 Samuel 6 tells

us that the Ark was called by His name (*I AM THAT I AM, Yahweh Sabaoth, God of the Angel Armies*) and that He Himself was enthroned between the cherubim carved on the lid. It was a holy object and a connection to Heaven itself. It was meant to be carried (not touched) via poles on men's shoulders. The presence of God is carried forth into the world by mankind, not by mechanism.

In addition, Uzzah was the grandson of Saul, a Benjamite. Transporting the holy things, including the Ark, was the privilege of the Levitical 'sons of Korah'. Uzzah was the wrong person with the wrong mechanism and, possibly, the wrong attitude.

The Lord has made fairly plain to us the things He has labelled 'wrong'. He has outlined the consequences for transgressing those boundaries. And so the 'kindling' of His anger, the space between the sparking incident and the fireball, can take anywhere between a few seconds to a few millennia.

> The *kindling* of God's anger can take *seconds* or *millennia*.

The Apocalypse is a case in point. It is not going to be a lovely day. People will die. A lot of people. People neither you nor I nor the Lord want to see perish. Again, we must remember that this is not God 'losing it.' This is God setting the scene for us in the Bible, begging us for several thousand years to make good choices (chief of all, choosing Him!) and then, finally, being true to His Word. What else can He do? I don't want to serve a God with no integrity and no backbone. If He says the wicked will have to perish, despite the fact

eleos
mercy, compassion

God had mercy on me so that Christ Jesus could use me as a prime example of His great patience with even the worst sinners.

1 Timothy 1:16 NLT

hypotypósin
pattern

hapasan makrothymian
perfect patience

that He has loved them and bought them dearly and wooed them with all He is and has – then that's not on Him.

It is an awesome miracle that He has already let human chaos go on as long as it has. Noah's generation should have been so lucky. If anything is going to demonstrate the immense patience of God, it's got to be the way He forbears to unleash firebolts every ten seconds. Instead, He gives us every chance to turn to Him. He gives us everything we need for life and godliness, every data point we need to escape wrath. To God, the Apocalypse is a tragedy waiting to happen. He takes no delight in the death of anyone, He tells us in Ezekiel 18:32. And yet He cannot suffer evil to live forever. Nahum 1:3 BSB captures both ends when it says, *'The Lord is slow to anger [erech 'appayim] and great in power; the Lord will by no means leave the guilty unpunished. His path is in the whirlwind and storm, and clouds are the dust beneath His feet.'* The implication – beyond the physical realities – is that while He may let the clouds gather, when He finally moves, He *really* moves.

 ## The Slow Burn

In the same way that God shows immense tolerance, we are called to bear with one another. We'll have more to dig up on this in *Core Values: Gentleness*, but for now, let's observe that though we may be prone to getting riled up, we reflect the nature of the Lord when we let things 'go through to the keeper.'

> *A servant of the Lord must not quarrel but must be kind to everyone, be able to teach, and be **patient** with difficult people. Gently instruct those who oppose the truth. Perhaps God will change those people's hearts, and they will learn the truth.*
>
> 2 Timothy 2:24–25 NLT

anexikakos — tolerant when provoked

It takes a long time to transform. We are being changed into the image of Christ *'with intensifying glory'* (BSB). It won't happen overnight, but it will happen – if we cooperate! 2 Corinthians 3:18 BLB shows us how: we become like whatever we fixate upon – *so let us continually behold Christ.* As we look at His glory we see who we can become in Him. And cyclically, as we look at who He is making us, we see the likeness of our Father making itself manifest.

> *And we all having been unveiled in face, beholding as in a mirror the glory of the Lord, are being transformed into the same image, from glory to glory, even as from the Lord, the Spirit.*
>
> 2 Corinthians 3:18 BLB

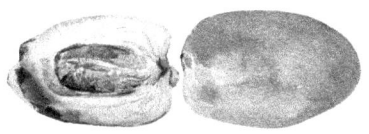

The Patience

GOD'S GIFT OF FREEWILL TO US has consequences for Him. Ultimately those consequences led to the death of Jesus for our salvation. Now the plans of God are never thwarted – though our freewill choices can have a serious impact on the timing when they come to pass.

After Elijah had fled from Jezebel and the death threats she was issuing, he ran to Mount Horeb – a journey of nearly seven weeks. God came to him there as a still small voice and gave him a set of instructions to carry out. One of these directives was to anoint an army commander named Hazael as the king of the neighbouring country of Aram.

But Elijah never got around to it, just as he never got around to fulfilling the second of God's directives: to anoint another army commander, Jehu, as king of Israel. Years later, Elijah went up in a whirlwind without accomplishing either of these tasks. And, at least in the second case, it's clear some negligence was involved since Jehu claimed he'd been a witness to the prophecy against Ahab after the murder of Naboth in order to confiscate his vineyard. That prophecy was delivered by Elijah and that means the two of them met up at some point but the opportunity to obey the Lord's command was allowed to slip on past.

A decade or so later, Elijah's protégé, Elisha, arranges for the anointing of Jehu – but then he follows the pattern of his mentor. Just as Elijah met up with Jehu and failed to anoint him, Elisha did the same thing when he met up with Hazael. He tells

Hazael he will be king and weeps for all the bloodshed that will occur as a result. But he doesn't fulfil the Lord's command to anoint Hazael.

Sometimes Scripture lets us know the 'might-have-beens' and gives us a glimpse of the patience of God in the process. The 'might-have-beens' are always most evident in the life of Jesus. As the Author and Perfector of our faith, He's the one who rewrites the story endings. We see Him do this – theologically it's called *recapitulation* – when He goes to the site of an ancient tragedy and upends the plotline.

Now back in the days of Elisha, Hazael murdered the king and took his throne as a result of what he was told by the prophet. But was that what God intended to happen?

I think we can look at the history of the early church and realise that God had incredible plans to the contrary.

Hazael's master, Ben Hadad, was named for the Canaanite storm-god, but he sent Hazael to inquire of a prophet of Yahweh. How amazing is that? This specific turning to Yahweh could have been the start of the Gentiles seeking God. However Elisha let the opportunity slip by when he failed, just as his mentor Elijah had done, to obey God and anoint the Lord's chosen.

Hazael was, after all, a brutal army commander from a foreign land who, at the behest of his ruler, was oppressing the Israelite people. His name means *God sees* or *vision of God*.

Seven or eight hundred years went by. Another army commander from another foreign land was in Israel at the behest of his ruler. He represented all that oppressed the Israelite people in the first century. And he saw a vision sent by God. Like Hazael coming to Elisha seeking to know more of God, this second army commander sent a delegation because he, too, wanted to know more of God — much, much more.

That second commander was the Roman centurion Cornelius.

Peter responded to the call when the delegation sent by Cornelius arrived. His assignment was to complete an unfinished task that went right back to the days of Elijah. On the surface, it looked like all God was asking for was that a foreign army commander be anointed. But in reality He was planning for a powerful visitation of the Spirit, not unlike the irruption that had happened to Saul on being anointed king.

God had been waiting patiently through the time of Elijah and his successor Elisha and his successor Jonah for the gathering of the Gentiles into His kingdom. Century after century after century He waited, offering opportunity after opportunity after opportunity for His prophets to choose to use their freewill in alignment with His heart, not with their biases.

I suspect it's much the same with us: generation after generation after generation He waits for someone to take up the mantle and fulfill the task of healing the tragic history of each individual family, as well as each nation.

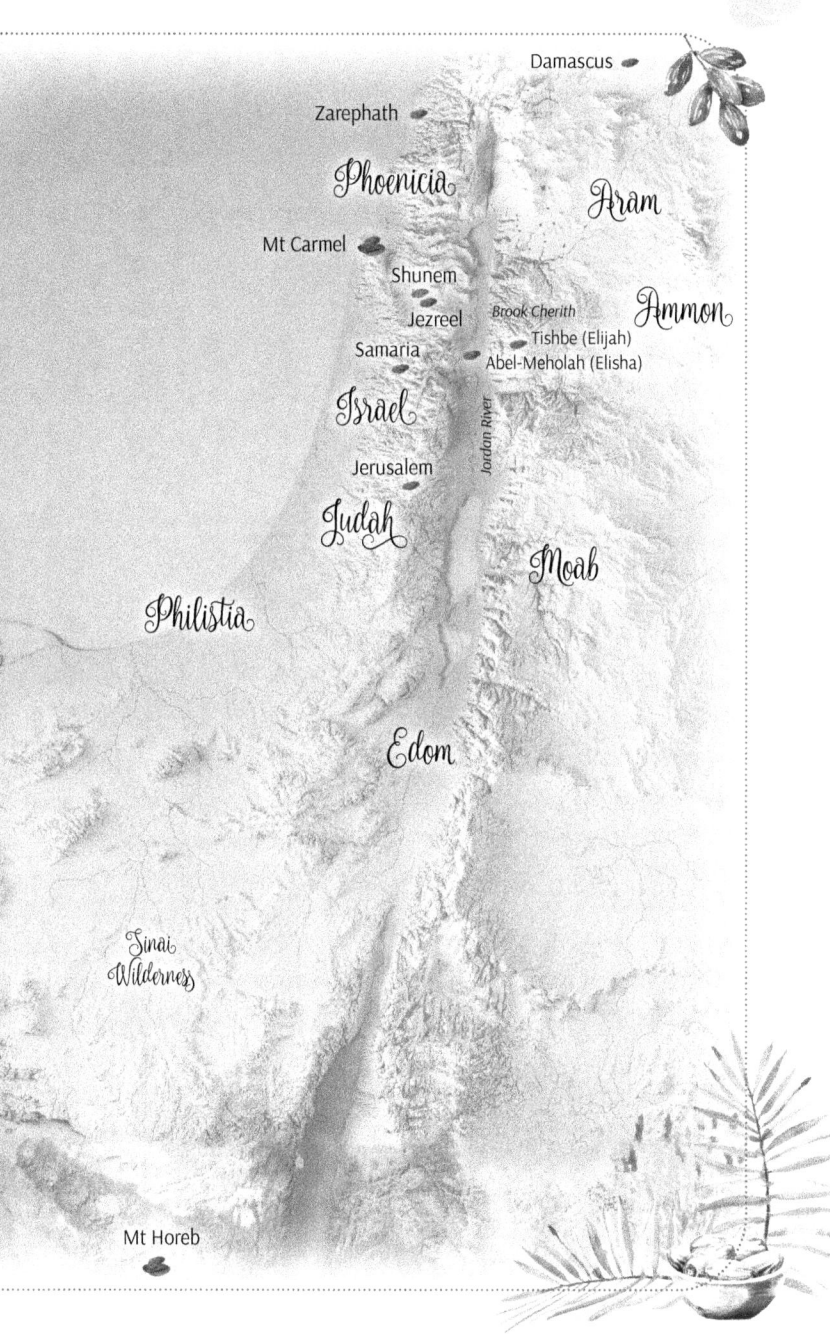

Junctions

Let's explore a few of the ways in which our fruit-words overlap and blend into one another. This is not an exhaustive list, of course — just a place to begin.

Patience and Love: Forbearance

Patience and love meet in *forbearance:* where our love for someone exerts a influence on the timing of whatever consequence they've got coming to them. This is true of God as well: He held the sins of the whole historical world in abeyance until the time was ripe for Jesus to carry them — and ours — on the cross. That is the most incredible piece of self-control you've ever heard of, especially when you consider the utter purity of God and His unreachable high standards.

And so forbearance, in the heart of God, is not only patience and love but also self-control and gentleness. Here I must gush in His praise! Words cannot express what a privilege it is to be on the receiving end of such a thing: that the high and lofty God — as towering and mind-blowingly complex to our humanity as we would be to a Lego minifig — that the Holy God, orders of magnitude above us, would condescend to *wait for us to turn to Him* for change. For *centuries*.

We are called to forbear with one another, too. God always has a plan (and several subsequent/consequent plans) for each relationship. He doesn't bend our partner, however; all of us are free to either cooperate with or rebel against His weaving. And so forbearance is not always rewarded in this life. Or, more accurately, it brings a reward within our own character — making us more godly people — even when it does not seem to 'succeed' in terms of influencing that of others. And though we may not see such reward within the relationship, we are called to employ patience through love nonetheless.

Patience and Joy: Hope

Patience and joy together birth *hope*.

There is a strained kind of anxious hope, which we experience in times of stress; but if we make Jesus our immediate refuge, we can hope in joyful anticipation. He's got us! This is very like faith, in fact. Separating 'faith' and 'hope' is like dividing between soul and spirit.

Forbear
= bear + for
= to **bear** things **for** someone's sake
= tolerate

For*e*bear
= bear + fore
= to be be**fore** you in the line of **bear**ing
= ancestor

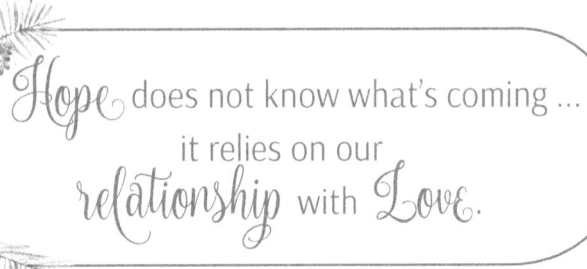

Hope does not know what's coming … it relies on our relationship with Love.

They hold hands, and it can be hard to know where the line is; but hope does not know what's coming, whereas faith does.

Hope relies entirely on our relationship with the Lord and our faith that He is love. When we are absolutely sure God is love and God is powerful, and that He is willing to extend that might on our behalf, then that is where we place our hope. We joy in who He is, the fact that He is love incarnate; we have patience that His timing is perfect; and this is different from faith, which is having a deep assurance in a specific predicted outcome. Our hope is in His *person*, not His *prophecy*. It can only be sustained by patience and joy, though (remembering that we're talking about one fruit with nine descriptors) they do bleed over into faith and peace.

All of these are the work of the Holy Spirit in us – not our natural patience (which reaches the end of its tether soon enough) nor our natural joy (which is a flash in the pan). Not our shakeable faith, nor our frangible peace. This is the deep river He flows through us by His Spirit, as He starts with His own presence and works in us over the years to incorporate these qualities into our nature and cause them to flourish.

Patience and Peace: Tranquillity

Patience and peace (wholebeing) meet in *tranquillity*. At maturity, peace grants an absolute confidence in God working all things together for our good, while patience allows us to rest in His perfect timing. Flapping becomes superfluous in such an environment of trust. Consider again that the Old French *paciente*, 'uncomplaining under misfortune' is so reminiscent of *pacific*, 'peaceful'. Tranquillity is being able to bear something without losing your peace over it.

Peace is also wise as well as serene. Melchizedek, king of Salem (*shalom*) was known as a great king and high priest, and Solomon (*shalom*) as the wisest of all. Together they spanned time from the patriarchal origins of Judaism to the end of the royal golden age. Together they contributed to the spiritual and physical genealogy of Jesus as our own High Priest and King.

There is a lot to be nervous about in history, including the varied nature of incidents befalling the people of God. He asks us to give Him our full trust, knowing the hairs on our heads are counted (Luke 12:7), but is blatantly honest about what that might entail: suffering. Rejection. Misfortune. Death. Also: reward. Covenant. Blessing. Inheritance. And legacy.

We do not know, going into this commitment, whether we will be like the Hebrews 11 faith-giants who *'escaped the edge of the sword'* in verse 34, or the other faith-giants, who were *'killed by the sword'* in verse 37. Despite the assertive way we cherry-pick and quote Scripture, there are no guarantees, and Jesus Himself warned that *'in this world you will have trouble'* (John 16:33 NIV). Our stance has to be like the three boys in the fiery furnace: 'God is able, but not obliged; either way, we're with Him.'

Tranquillity trusts God to keep the overarching plan of history and prophecy on track, and also to fold us into it in a way that renders us treasured partners, not grist. We may be pawns rather than kings

– bishops and knights at the most – but His eye has always been on the sparrow. No pawn falls without His hand extended to them, even underlying them. His salvation is a safety net even when we are far from safe.

> *The steps of a good man are ordered/established by the LORD,*
> *And He delights in his way.*
> *Though he fall, he shall not be utterly cast down;*
> *For the LORD upholds him with His hand.*

Psalm 37:23–24 NKJV

> *…. all the days ordained for me were written in Your book before one of them came to be.*

Psalm 139:16b NIV

> *There is no one like the God of Jeshurun,* — 'the dear, upright people' of Israel
> *who rides across the heavens to help you*
> *and on the clouds in His majesty.*
> *The eternal God is your refuge,*
> *and underneath are the everlasting arms.*

Deuteronomy 33:26–27a NIV

When we consider 'peace' in the sense of interpersonal peace – between humanity and God – then adding patience to the mix demonstrates just how committed God is to His relationship with us. He is forever trying, again and again, to turn our faces back toward Him. If you have ever seen Brad Jersak's brilliant video clip *The Gospel in Chairs*, you'll be familiar with the concept. Every time we move away, God takes steps to close the gap.

- He was close in the Garden, and we chose forbidden knowledge.
  He promised a Saviour.
- He shepherded Israel, and they chose idols.
  He sent them prophets.

- He gave us His personal name, and we labelled Him 'the Name.'
  He sent a Person.
- He gave us His Son, and we turned to His mother.
  He gave us the Holy Spirit.

We talk about 'inviting Jesus into your heart.' Seldom do we stop to realise that the entire Bible shows God inviting US into HIS heart.

Patience and Kindness: Grace

The best description I can find for the meeting of patience and kindness is *grace*. In truth, 'grace' in its *poikilos* ('many-coloured') array could apply for the entire description of the fruit of the Spirit. However – without limiting grace down to just the two things – this is a very good place to write about it.

Patience waits, without hurry, in readiness to act; kindness has proactive deeds to enact when the time is right.

Grace is the unmerited favour of God:

God's **R**iches **A**t **C**hrist's **E**xpense.

It means He enfolds and blesses and empowers us regardless of whether we think we deserve it or not. The ticket into the grace of God is faith; but, turn about, the fact that we even *have* faith is a gift from God in His grace. Everything dovetails into who He is. Literally, 'All is gift,' as Ignatius of Loyola said.

God's grace chooses to look at the faith we have in Jesus and His atonement, rather than looking at our sins or achievements. His enabling grace also gives us the strength to say *no* to sin, and to attain achievements. And when we extend grace to others, it's often in the form of believing in the other person's potential regardless of where they're currently at. God doesn't 'not see' how poor our behaviour is; He just uses a different metric to quantify our status. Sometimes, He extends incredible grace to us in our least deserving moments.

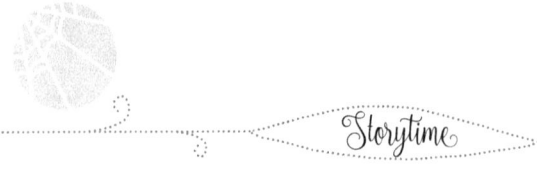

You think Him graceless. His words are harsh, you say; but I was there, I was their recipient, and I tell you — there is none more gracious than He. Let me share with you the full story.

We were desperate. My boy, he has a disability. He suffers from panolepsy. It causes pandemonium inside him. You think I use that word lightly; but I don't. I mean it literally. Pan. Demon. Ium. His whole life he's had seizures — not just the kind that make a person absent, or rigid, or trembling. We got the trifecta. My boy's seizures are literally like something seizes his body and mind, sending both out of control. He flails and screams and gnashes his teeth. He foams and shakes violently. He throws himself into the fire or water, as if he wants to end it all. It's frankly terrifying. Only our love for him keeps us from hightailing it out of there. There are occasional moments of respite when my sweet boy emerges, broken and helpless, still unable to speak; but on the whole, it's getting worse. Both body and soul are deteriorating horribly. And it's breaking our hearts. He's fourteen.

At first we took him to the Temple, when he was little. They were quick enough to tell us that he was afflicted by an evil spirit. Well, duh. But they said there was nothing they could do. Casting out demons was the Messiah's forte, they said; and do you see a Messiah anywhere around here? No. Go home, they said. Repent of everything you can think of. Come back and offer the appropriate sacrifices. And make a donation. Maybe God will intervene; but we've never seen it, they said. Not even the great and prophetic King Saul could shed a demon.

Well, that was about as helpful as a fishing net for a ceiling. We tried all that. Nothing. We attempted to be patient, but it just wasn't working.

So, we fished around for another approach. Clearly, this kind of panic — *pan-olepsy* — comes from Pan. As much as the idea of getting

involved with Pan/Azazel the Scapegoat made the hairs on our arms stand up, it was already involved with us. If sacrificing to the Lord wasn't going to help, maybe we could placate the driving spirit itself somehow, get it to let up a bit. Pay protection money, if you like. Any improvement would be way ahead of none.

The more we examined this idea, the more credence we gave it. I know, stupid; but it's the place we were in. We didn't stop to think that maybe other consequences would ensue. Like that it wouldn't be a one-time deal; we'd have to keep on paying. We'd have invited the thing into covenant with our family. And it would put paid to any covenant protection the Lord might still wish to give our household. I'd like to say I had no idea at the time what a big deal that really was … but that would be a lie. I went down this road on purpose. By the time we actually *met* the Lord, we were long gone.

We trekked all the way north to Panias, that the Romans call Caesarea Philippi. It was rough going — days and weeks of walking over all terrain, struggling with carrying my gangly son, whose demon tantrummed and taunted and rolled him away with exasperating regularity. I don't know if it saw what was coming, or it merely amped up the pressure to get us all more firmly into Azazel's clutches. It was hell, just getting to the Gates of Hell.

Yeah, that's what they call it, the shrine of Pan at the base of Mount Hermon. There's an underground river, and huge gaping mouths, hungry for offerings and repellent acts. The people who hang around are fully pagan. By then, so were we. The theory was that if you did the right (very wrong) rituals, you could petition Hell for relief. Maybe.

None of that helped either. If Azazel was there, it was enjoying the whole thing; my son's exploitation did not ease one whit. We kept trying; it kept not working. Hell was laughing at us.

And then along came a really big band of people. Two of them stopped to talk to us, and it quickly became apparent they

were followers of a rabbi named Yeshua. A rabbi with a difference: apparently he'd given them authority (what? how? unless he was the Messiah, haha?) to cast out demons and heal the sick.

So I shrugged and led them into the little house we'd rented, and showed them my son, defiantly. They put their hands on his shoulders, and the demon writhed and made its usual inarticulate noises, only louder and more panicked than usual. They prayed. The demon shut up, all right, but it refused to leave, *and how!*

They seemed puzzled, like they'd actually expected a different result. They tried again. And just like everything else we'd given a shot — it didn't work. They looked at each other, perplexed and a little afraid. And they mumbled their condolences, and left, saying that Yeshua himself would be along presently. Whatever power they thought they'd had, it clearly wasn't as big as Azazel's. A new wave of hopelessness swamped me.

I really, really, really needed a *real* Messiah.

From Yahweh.

Nothing else was going to do it.

I know there's nothing in the Law or the Prophets that says the Messiah will be able to cast out demons. But some of the rabbis claim an old tradition that He'll even have the ability to expel deaf-and-dumb ones. Besides, there's nothing that says He'll be able to magically multiply food, either, and I heard a really strange rumour out of Galilee about that, not long ago. There was just the tiniest chance that the scribes were wrong, and there really *was* a Messiah about.

What if this rabbi *can* help? Oh, but His delegates couldn't. What's the point in asking? *But what's the point in NOT asking?*

I went 'round and 'round this dilemma for a week, while my son thrashed and convulsed and moaned and ground his teeth down some more. I was done with Pan. The goat-demon wasn't interested in helping; at least that Yeshua's disciples, for all their incompetence, had given it a go!

And finally he arrived. Not from the road, but from the mountain.

My son had caused a scene (again). A group had gathered, as they do when there's a spectacle, the vultures! I explained what I was doing there. Nobody looked askance at me; they were all in Panias for the same thing, after all – spiritual intervention. Any kind, really.

So when four figures were seen trudging down the sacred mountain where the gods of the nations were said to live, the crowd rushed to see who they were. Why were their faces shining? Was it a trick of the light? Which one of them was the rabbi? Why would a rabbi be *here?*

It turned out to be the nondescript one the other three gave deference to, not the big surly one or the thunderous-looking pair, who would have been my first choices.

I shouted. He heard me. He listened. He got angry. I deserved it. He knew full well what it meant, me and my boy being at Panias, the *Pan-shrine*, in the first place. This was not a place where people sought Yahweh. I had some nerve, even approaching him. But I was all out of options, and ready to try God again, in the final extremity.

And Rabbi Yeshua? 'How long do I have to put up with this kind of unbelieving deviance?' he demanded. 'Seeking Azazel? Seriously?' But then he lowered his voice and started asking more concerned questions. We both knew the Lord God had been putting up with spiritual perversity for a very, very long time, though not without warnings. For all his outburst, Yeshua wasn't turning his back and leaving, which surprised me. Nor was he throwing rocks. He had a little patience left in him, and a lot of kindness also. So maybe God did, too ...

And finally he was ready to see my boy.

Well, the demon did not like that one little bit. It was only going to let go over my son's dead body. It threw him down with a full display of its horrible powers, as if to kill him right in front of Life.

And this told me one thing: whatever was in Yeshua was the opposite of what was in my son. It. Felt. *Threatened*. Finally!

Yeshua did not look worried. I couldn't be sure what he was feeling; there were fleeting expressions of sadness, indignation, but overriding all of that, in the end ... compassion.

'Can you do anything?' I pleaded.

'*Can* I? All things are possible to him who believes!' Did He mean his own belief, or mine? Or both? *ALL* things? *Truly?* Was this ... it?

I burst into tears. 'I do believe!' I wanted to. But he could see right through me. I switched to total honesty. 'Help my unbelief!' I wailed.

The crowd was thickening. He wasted no more time.

He rebuked the spirit.

It reacted, violently.

And ... it left.

There was silence. My boy lay in the dirt. He looked dead – his atrophied, scarred limbs splayed out, unmoving. Had the demon taken my son's spirit to the underworld? That's what everyone was wondering. Was this the price paid for its eviction?

But Yeshua ignored them, all his focus on my boy. He reached down and grabbed his hand. My son lifted his head, and the crowd gasped. He fixed his eyes on Yeshua, clear of gaze. Yeshua's lips quirked up and he gave a tug. And my son ... who hadn't walked since ... ever ... folded one leg under his body, and levered himself up with the other. And he stood up. And they grinned at each other. Then they looked at me, and my son said, 'Abba!'

And I – I sat down suddenly in the dirt and cried like a baby. For I had received a miracle: my faithlessness had been met with divine condescension. I deserved nothing from God – but He gave anyway. Because love cares, and grace stoops.

Patience and Goodness: Fortitude

Fortitude is a wonderful word-picture for the kind of moral courage that is as strong as a fort. How do we get *courage* out of patience and goodness? Glad you asked.

Patience, as we know, is that which is unhurried. Goodness, we will argue in the next volume, is that which is full of virtue. And so picture this: a state of being which is like a castle, rich and content, well-fortified, happy to wait out whatever besieges it. This 'caer' has cast all its cares on its King. It is well-provisioned, generous to others, integrous in its construction, and — in the strength of the King's superb administration — self-sufficient. It fears not the night terrors, nor the daily arrows, nor the darkness-stalking pestilence, nor the midday plague (Psalm 91). It doesn't *like* war or adversity, but it's well-situated to withstand them. Nobody enjoys being in pain. But if we copy the patience of the Holy Spirit, and draw upon the goodness of the Father, we are that much more able to display the flint-brow of the Son, even when thorns encircle it.

Remember, these are *ideal* virtues. God does not expect you to be Superman. He is the only Hero in the room! But as you live in the shelter of the Most High, He holds out His arsenal for you to use, while your partnership with Him gradually permits osmosis to take place in your life.

Patience and Faith: Tenacity

Hebrews 6:12 talks about inheriting the promises we hope for through faith and patience. The chapter, as a whole (overleaf) talks about other fruit you will find in the life of a mature, love-living believer who has graduated from Christianity 101. 'Works and rites won't get you to Heaven,' it says, 'but that doesn't mean God doesn't appreciate a good and loving work ethic. Keep on applying

Therefore let us leave the elementary teachings about Christ and go on to maturity, not laying again the foundation of repentance from dead works [acts that lead to death], and of faith in God, instruction about baptisms [cleansing rites], the laying on of hands, the resurrection of the dead, and eternal judgment. And this we will do, if God permits.

It is impossible for those who have once been enlightened, who have tasted the heavenly gift, who have shared in the Holy Spirit, who have tasted the goodness of the word of God and the powers of the coming age – and then have fallen away – to be restored to repentance, because they themselves are crucifying the Son of God all over again and subjecting Him to open shame.

For land that drinks in the rain often falling on it and that produces a crop useful to those for whom it is tended receives the blessing of God. But land that produces thorns and thistles is worthless, and its curse is imminent. In the end it will be burned.

Even though we speak like this, beloved, we are convinced of better things in your case—things that accompany salvation. For God is not unjust. He will not forget your work and the love you have shown for His name as you have ministered to the saints and continue to do so.

6 BSB

> **spoudēn**
> speed, diligence, haste, earnestness, enthusiasm

> **elpidos**
> hope, expectation, confidence, trust

*We want each of you to show this same diligence to the very end, in order to make your hope sure. Then you will not be sluggish, but will imitate those who through **faith and patience** inherit what has been promised.*

> **nōthroi**
> sluggish, slothful, lazy, inert, lackadaisical, listless, dull

> **pisteōs**
> faith, belief, trust, confidence

> **makrothymias**
> longsuffering

*When God made His promise to Abraham, since He had no one greater to swear by, He swore by Himself, saying, "I will surely bless you and multiply your descendants." (Genesis 22:17) And so Abraham, after **waiting patiently**, obtained the promise.*

> **makrothymēsas**
> to be long-spirited

Men swear by someone greater than themselves, and their oath serves as a confirmation to end all argument. So when God wanted to make the unchanging nature of His purpose very clear to the heirs of the promise, He guaranteed it with an oath. Thus by two unchangeable things in which it is impossible for God to lie, we who have fled to take hold of the hope set before us may be strongly encouraged.

We have this hope as an anchor for the soul, firm and secure. It enters the inner sanctuary behind the curtain, where Jesus our forerunner has entered on our behalf. He has become a high priest forever in the order of Melchizedek.

that in your love for one another and for Him. The exercise'll keep you healthy.'

Diligence (*spoudēn*) is contrasted with sluggishness (*nōthroi*). Diligence is a cousin to patience, is it not? They are both in it for the long haul, working tirelessly and integrously through the tedium until the reward emerges. Sluggishness, on the other hand, can't see the point. It resists patience, not via brash action but via indifference. It has no investment.

Service to one another is a sign of love for Jesus's name, says verse 10. People, as we know, do not always present as delightful. They (we!) can be arrogant, whiny, touchy, excuse-ridden — hard to love. And yet, God manages to love us. The name 'Jesus' means *God saves*. When we love Jesus, love *God Saves*, it becomes easier to serve others lovingly. We start to see them as *people God went to extreme lengths to save*.

Scripture has a lot to say about tenacity, endurance and perseverance. It has as much to say about God's perseverance as it does about ours. Yahweh is a most tenacious God. He will not let your foot slip (Psalm 121:3) and no one can snatch you out of His hand (John 10:28). He will let you run as far as you choose, and depending on your Individual Education Plan, He will either wait for you to come to your senses or actively chase you down. He will not rest until He has exhausted every possibility of bringing your church, your heart and your life to culmination (Philippians 1:6).

So how does tenacity arise from combining patience with faith? Simple. Patience is content to let things take as long as necessary, while faith refuses to let go of the promises of God. The latter are the pot of gold at the end of the rainbow, and it doesn't really matter how long the rainbow is. '*Let us not become weary in doing good,*' Galatians 6:9 NIV encourages us, '*for at the proper time we will reap a harvest if we do not give up.*'

Isaiah 28:16 talks about the security of building on Jesus as our foundation:

> *I lay a stone in Zion, a tested stone,*
> *a precious cornerstone for a sure foundation;*
> *the one who relies on it will never be stricken with panic* (NIV)
> *whoever believes will not act hastily* (NKJV)
> *Whoever believes need never be shaken.* (NLT)

The Lord is to be our wreath, our crown; our well-supplied fortress, and the strength of our defenders; our rest, instead of our *to-do* list; the truth on which we stand. When we have those things, we can make solid decisions based on faith in what God has promised. We aren't rattled into action by FOMO (fear of missing out) but place our trust in His good judgment on what is best for us, and when.

Patience and Gentleness: Even Temper

'Gentleness' is the item on the Spirit-fruit list that gets the greatest variation in rendering. By the time you distill *prautes* down from 'gentleness/meekness/mildness,' you might be surprised to find 'humility' at the bottom of it all. Yet all of these descriptors roll so well with patience to produce a person who fails to flare up under ongoing provocation.

Such a person becomes difficult to manipulate. You cannot prosecute a war of attrition against someone who has infinite patience (even if it is borrowed from the Spirit!). They will simply wait you out, because waiting is much less of a hardship when one is allied with God and His promises.

Such a person is not at the whim of ego. They don't need it built up or defended; they don't need it displayed. A person of true humility does not really think about whether or not they are Being

Humble; they simply forget, or habitually decline, to fly their flag. The only way you could provoke a gentle person is by threatening not their own pride, but the wellbeing of another. They may yet be a person of great justice, but they are less likely to be forceful about it. Such souls tend to the dogged rather than the dramatic.

Jesus, no matter how dense He sometimes found others, never lost His temper. If you immediately think of the scene where He cleared the Temple, consider this. Scripture says He took some cords and braided a whip. So, it could not have been a case of 'Jesus walked in one day and totally lost it.' Rather, He came in one particular day, after several years of visiting without comment. This time, He came with intent. Perhaps He brought the cords with Him, perhaps He found them there; but regardless, He then took the time to sit or stand there and calmly plait them.

Nobody noticed, I'm guessing. The place was raucous – this area which had been designated for Gentiles to come and seek Him. *No, we don't want those lowlife goyim in here. They don't matter.* Though neither Moses nor Solomon mandated a separate court for women or Gentiles, Herod's temple had both ... ostensibly. But this space thumbed its nose at its formal designation. It was filled with moneychangers issuing demon-engraved coins to fleece the Jews seeking to get right with God. It was full of sacrificial livestock available only at inflated prices. The left-of-centre rabbi in the corner playing with something in His hands might not have garnered much attention. Then again ... the merchants closest to Him perhaps wondered, 'What's that guy planning on doing with that? He'd better not come near my stock.' Nobody dreamed that, in cold blood, He might start systematically turning over tables and swinging the rope.

Did He flick it at the merchants, or at the livestock? If you were there with ten or so valuable top-quality beasts strung together, and they started stampeding toward the gate – of course you'd run out after them. Jesus wasn't necessarily trying to make people bleed; He

was simply trying to get them *out*. It was supposed to be a place of prayer. In a weird sense, it could be by *these* stripes — the ones He inflicted in the Outer Court that day — that we are healed and able to be truly reconciled to God without endless animal sacrifice. Or was He foreshadowing and preempting His own scourging? Tit for tat.

Consider that Jesus, as Trinity member, was the Maker of the world. *'God created everything through Him, and nothing was created except through Him.'* (John 1:3 NLT) He was the designer of the Tabernacle and thus, later, the first Temple. So in one sense, He is experiencing *Look what they've done to My House, Dad!* And yet He does not scream at them ... He simply takes premeditated action. He is not, apparently, thinking about His rights as designer or Great High Priest or even rabbi. He knows who He is. He is thinking about His Father's purposes.

'The anger of man does not produce the righteousness of God,' writes His brother in James 1:20 ESV. While Jesus uses pointed words at times, there is no evidence that He delivered them in a snarl or a roar. Isaiah 42:2 NIV says, *'He will not shout or cry out, or raise His voice in the streets.'* The only record we have of Jesus getting loud was when He stood up indoors at the Feast and called out, *'If anyone is thirsty, let him come to Me and drink'* (an offer of generous mercy, not a telling-off) in John 7:37 BSB. And so He may well have been cool, calm and collected even when calling out the *'brood of vipers'*: a deadpan assessment, if you will. He had no need to assert Himself, and even seemed to avoid doing so.

Proverbs 14:17 has warnings about temper, variously rendered:

He that is soon angry dealeth foolishly	**KJV**
A short-tempered person acts stupidly	**GW**
The hotheaded do things they'll later regret	**MSG**

'Even temper', however, isn't necessarily limited in definition to 'not volatile'. There is an evenness of demeanour which could be contrasted with, say, a person whose mood swings from one extreme

to the other. An even temper would not swing so strongly. A gentle spirit would wax cool and warm, rather than freezing or burning. *'I wish you were either hot or cold'* is likely, writes Dr Paul Ellis, to be referring to choosing a system of relating to God: Law or grace. It is not in any form a licence to growl or spit.

The godliness of an even temperament does not mean that if you suffer from manic depression, you're out of the will of God. It simply means you need Him more because the physical odds are particularly stacked against you. And He is not at all against you receiving medical/psychological treatment as well as spiritual aid. Medicine and confession are both inventions of His, and *'with many counsellors comes deliverance'* (Proverbs 11:14 BSB).

Worry is another thorn in the side of equilibrium. One of our key texts about anxiety is Philippians 4. Yet every time I've heard the passage quoted, the orator has glossed quickly over *'Let your gentleness be evident to all. The Lord is near,'* as if it were a strange sort of pilcrow after the buoyant *'Rejoice!'* Then we skip happily to the bit we all came for: *'prayer and petition.'* But what if the passage was intended to be read, not just as, 'Take heart!' but also as, 'Chill out!' And what if the next line should be read like this? …

The Lord is near. So do not be anxious about anything.
[Pause.]

That puts a whole new slant on it. We aren't to separate joy, gentleness and trust, but to joyfully trust *within* the context of

> We are able to *let go of anxiety* because *the Lord is near* to us.

Patience with God's timing relies on our trust in Him.

having our gentle Paraclete and Example at our back. We aren't told 'stop worrying' without context. The context is that the Lord is near to us at all times.

Anxiety is obviously the enemy of peace, but it is also the enemy of patience, and thus of trust. Anxiety tells us that God isn't going to show up on time, or that some crucial detail will have been overlooked. Anxiety, as a psychological condition, is not quite the same thing as worry; it's more like a state of being *staked out for* worry. It's not technically a sin, and it's not mentioned in the 'acts of the flesh.' But it is most definitely a hindrance, and perhaps even an insult to the love of God. Even this knowledge can compound things, because now we are not only anxious about the issue but anxious about the need to repent of being anxious. All of this needs to come under the grace of God's immense understanding. When we are in such a spiritual battle, all of these thoughts must be rounded up and surrendered to the knowledge of God's character and love.

I would like to tell you to cast all your cares on the Lord and it will all go away. But no such promise is made. We cast our cares on Him and hang on like grim life. And, in response, He holds on right back, feeding His peace into us. Sometimes it's a trickle, and sometimes a flood. He understands our weaknesses — not academically, but empathetically. He does not hold such frailty against us. St Paul talked about the daily burden of the welfare of the fledgling church network. He spoke of inwardly burning. And yet … God was able to use him, despite his all-too-human weaknesses. He can use us, too.

Patience and Self-Control: Restraint

Proverbs 16:32 NIV declares,

> 'Better a patient person than a warrior,
> one with self-control
> than one who takes a city.'

erech 'appayim — slow to anger, long-breathing

umoshel beruchow — one who rules his own spirit

The Septuagint has this, *'It's better to be forgiving than strong.'* How can you rule a city if you can't rule yourself? God, it seems, would prefer us to capture our emotions and behaviour rather than towns. This has profound implications for 'take this city for Christ!' evangelism. *Of course* we want revival in our cities. But God primarily wants each of us to be conformed to the image of Christ. And in His eyes it is a great tragedy when one of us ushers in a great move of God, but falls by the wayside in the process. He rejoices over every sinner who repents. But He also grieves over every former penitent who returns to sin. It's no good trying to please Him with numbers. You are one of those numbers. If love for one's neighbour is bringing them close to Christ, then don't forget that you're to love your neighbour *as yourself*. Be careful to stay close to Christ yourself!

Christ is a perfect picture of restraint. His patience with the disciples, the crowds, the children, the desperate was legendary. His self-control in the face of indignation-rousing hypocrisy was amazing. I wonder just how much restraint it required to stay mangled and nailed to that terrible cross for hours on end. He knew He could have called Heaven and cried, 'I'm a celebrity … get Me out of here!' But He did not. He endured every ugly minute until all of our debt was paid.

God is ultimate power and, like the biggest guy in the neighbourhood, can 'take us' any time. He chooses not to. He is not a bully, but a parent. His patience has huge areas of overlap with His self-control. He doesn't lash out at us. He does give us enough rope; but He clearly enunciates the right path to avoid a hanging.

# Perseverance

In the long run (and there is no other kind, really) perseverance and patience are all about answering the questions, *What do you really want?* and *How much do you want it?*

Any tertiary or quaternary student knows that, other than love of learning, the thing that keeps one going to the end of one's course is the shining goal: qualification and publication. Anyone saving for a house deposit, a new outfit, a trip, a technological item, or retirement understands the principle of delayed gratification. What we want *now* must come second to what we want *ultimately*. Perseverance in saving requires a great deal of self-control and hope. Perseverance while we are *being* saved is the same. It pulls something out of us we didn't know we had. It employs expectation and desire and anticipation to keep us stayed to the course. In many ways, it's a powerful demonstration of faith: pitting all of one's actions toward a yet-to-be-seen outcome.

I do believe that this is something the Lord shares with us. While we are persevering with our faith despite adversity — as the world 'has fun' around us — He has persevered in living a completely sinless life, and continues to persevere in His endless efforts to tame the wild in us.

I stand in awe of people who have been forced to suffer for their faith. I am madly in love with Jesus Christ, but the tests this love has weathered are tame compared to those endured by the saints beyond the historical, Iron and Bamboo Curtains. Foxe's *Book of Martyrs* is the stuff of nightmares. *What do you really want?* Christ, truth, and salvation. *How much do you want it?* Enough to be tortured to death for it.

I grew up as a missionaries' kid, and from the age of about 8 was exposed to the idea that following Jesus could have awful consequences. What I learned about suffering for the Lord was not

age-appropriate, but what it *did* do for me was check any idea that Christianity was escapism for the faint of heart.

These people were hardcore. Either they loved the Lord a lot more than I did, or they had a greater revelation of Him. Yet perhaps they were people like me, earnest but weak — but they had a strong God who carried them *in extremis*, and maybe a grace-given doggedness to follow Him even if He did *not* carry them. I do not believe that, as a class, they suffered no pain, though I do believe that in some cases the Lord mitigated the pain, or appeared to them during the pain. I do not believe their sufferings were punishments, as that would negate the power of the Blood to wash away sin. I do believe we need to be ready to suffer for our faith if we are ever called upon to do so. We know the Kingdom-rock grows into a mountain that fills the earth — but we do not know *when.* And if it is not this side of the Second Coming, this world as a whole will remain antagonistic toward us and under the sway of the enemy.

'Endure hardship as disclipline,' says Hebrews 12:7 NIV. Make good use of what comes your way. Lean into it, let it teach you what it can. Allow God to make a lesson of it. Suffering produces perseverance, which produces character — all in the context of the Holy Spirit coursing His love through us. Sometimes, He lovingly brings such lessons to us. Other times, they come of their own accord and, with great mastery, He upcycles them for us. In all cases we can hold onto Romans 8:28 NIV:

> *And we know that in all things*
> *God works for the good of those who love Him,*
> *who have been called according to His purpose.*

Many of the Scriptures where the English translation is given as 'perseverance' or 'endurance' turn out to be *hypomonen*. There is, however, another word for this virtue:

*Pray at all times in the Spirit with every prayer and request, and stay alert with all **perseverance** and intercession for all the saints.*

Ephesians 6:18 CSB

proskarterēsis
persistence, steadfastness, strong perseverance which prevails by interacting with God

The CJB gives it as *'vigilantly and persistently'*. This is a specific instruction related to prayer. Be informed, be focused, be relentless – but above all, be entwined!

Make every effort to add to your

Faith

Goodness

and

Knowledge

We also glory in our sufferings, because we know that

and

Suffering

Self-Control

produces

and

Romans 5:3-5   *Perseverance*   2 Peter 1:5-8

produces   and

Character   *Godliness*

produces   and

Hope   *Mutual Affection*

↑   and

Vindication   *Love*

↑   ↑

Holy Spirit   *Effectiveness, Productivity*

↑   ↑

God's Love   *Knowledge of Christ*

A Little While

What does the Lord mean by 'in a little while'? Surely, His perspective is unlike ours.

In some of the verses opposite, 'a little while' can mean a couple of hours, and in others, a couple of millennia. Perhaps the most sensible conclusion we can draw is that whatever God calls 'a little while,' by comparison the Eternal Kingdom must be vaster, more immanent and eminent, than we can imagine.

And so, He asks us to join Him in being patient in the meantime. Both He and we are working and waiting, watching and whiling away the time. Time is God's tool, not His master: He is outside time. Jesus did not know when He would be back, but He said 'in a little while,' and the hearers thought He meant in their lifetime. In a fortunate twist of linguistics, 'generation', 'age' and 'race' are all valid interpretations of the word *genea* used in Matthew 24:34: *'Truly I tell you, this* genea [and My words] *will certainly not pass away* [though heaven and earth will] *until all these things* [of distress and the Second Coming] *have happened.'* Of course it is technically possible that He was including Himself in that generation, for while He did indeed die, He never permanently passed away!

Trying God's Patience

God has an infinite supply of forbearance, but that doesn't mean it isn't taxed from time to time. Consider the story of the king with no vision in Isaiah 7:10–14 NKJ.

> *The Lord [Yahweh] spoke again to Ahaz, saying, 'Ask a sign for yourself from the Lord your God [Yahweh Eloheka]; ask it either in the depth or in the height above.'*

Speaker & Reference	Verse	Duration
Job: Job 24:24	*For a little while [the wicked] are exalted, and then they are gone …*	120 years
David: Psalm 37:10	*A little while, and the wicked will be no more …*	3 millennia +
Isaiah: Isaiah 26:20	*… hide yourselves for a little while until His [Apocalyptic] wrath has passed by.*	7 years
Isaiah: Isaiah 63:18	*For a little while Your people possessed Your holy place …*	430 years
God: Ezekiel 11:16	*Although I sent them far away … yet for a little while I have been a sanctuary for them in the countries where they have gone.*	5 years
God: Haggai 2:6	*In a little while I will once more shake the heavens and the earth …*	25 centuries
Jesus: John 12:35	*You are going to have the light just a little while longer.*	a few hours
Jesus: John 16:16	*'In a little while you will see Me no more, and then after a little while you will see Me.'*	a weekend
poss. Priscilla: Hebrews 2:9	*… Jesus, who was made lower than the angels for a little while, now crowned with glory and honour …*	33 years
poss. Priscilla: Hebrews 10:37	*In just a little while, He who is coming will come and will not delay.*	2 millennia
Peter: 1 Peter 1:6	*In all this you greatly rejoice, though now for a little while you may have had to suffer grief in all kinds of trials.*	20 years

But Ahaz said, 'I will not ask, nor will I test the LORD!'

*Then He said, 'Hear now, O house of David! Is it a small thing for you to **weary** men, but will you **weary** my God [Elohay] also? Therefore the Lord [Adonai] Himself will give you a sign: Behold, the virgin shall conceive and bear a Son, and shall call His name Immanuel.*

> *laah*
> become impatient, exhausted, parched, find difficulty

The question must be asked: why didn't King Ahaz want a sign from God? Was it because he had no confidence in God's power, or was there another reason?

Ahaz ruled the Kingdom of Judah and was 12th in descent from David. He was young and evil. He not only sacrificed his son to idols and defied the proper worship of God, but he stripped/renovated/vandalised/syncretised His Temple.

There is the slightest chance that Isaiah was being snide when he used the phrase *'the LORD your God.'* Ahaz didn't own Yahweh as his God, or at least not solely. God may have been reminding Ahaz that He was God anyway, which Isaiah backed up by switching to '<u>my</u> God.' Or (much less likely) He may have been taunting Ahaz into asking for a sign from one of his helpless idols, knowing that from sky to pit, from Sheol to Shammayim, they could give him nothing.

Ahaz was not a man in good relationship with Yahweh. He wasn't even in good relationship with Israel, having more in common with the dangerous Assyrians by that point. It was a miracle Isaiah, who had already survived two better kings and would see a fourth, would even talk to him. People who know they are not on God's side do not expect God to be on theirs. This is a kind of abstract humility, I suppose, or at least wry realism. But they have forgotten the character of God. He longs to be gracious to us! Romans 15:5–6 refers to Him as *'the God of hypomonēs and paraklēseōs'* – endurance and encouragement.

The Lord got so tired of waiting for Ahaz to 'come good' like his ancestor and get a clue, that He issued the most astounding prophecy of all time without being asked. This speaks to the vast generosity of the Lord. He wants to give us something good; we can't be bothered to turn up and ask for it. But even when we are at our densest and darkest, He is still at His most extravagant!

> *Therefore the Lord **waits**
> to be gracious to you,
> and therefore He exalts Himself
> to show mercy to you.*
>
> *For the Lord is a God of justice;
> blessed are all **those who wait for** Him.*
>
> Isaiah 30:18 ESV

chakah — to wait, tarry, or long for

howke — those who long for

The lie we're offered: 'God has had enough!'

Knowing the infinity of God's very composition, you would think we wouldn't fall for this fib so often. But it can be awkward trying to separate out the mental concepts of 'my father' and 'my Heavenly Father'.

Human fathers reach a limit. Try them once too often, and you may be snapped at, or be on the receiving end of other unpleasant consequences. Most fathers are genuinely trying to do the best they can with the resources available to them on that particular day. Most are trying, in fact, to be good dads for the long haul, and not simply

reactionary in the moment. But they know — you and I know — this doesn't always go to plan.

Our Heavenly Father is not like that. *'My thoughts/ways are higher than yours,'* He informs us in Isaiah 55:8–9. And how! As we've noted, it can take *centuries* for God to have 'had enough,' even when we actually wish it otherwise. None of us, at this juncture, are living for centuries. God is not going to lose His temper with us. He is most certainly not going to walk out on us, nor even wish to.

That doesn't mean He doesn't experience emotional frustration, though in God, frustration is never something that overpowers His other emotions. Those emotions may be deeper than ours, as a moving object is deeper than a pencil dot, but they are uniquely balanced in God. The wrath of God is not a powder keg that explodes out of Him randomly. It seems to me less like a volcano going off, and more like a slow cooker. It has a scheduled release time, and slowly builds to a simmer. There are warning markers — millennia of them — to tell us that it will, eventually, reach a rolling boil. But even then, I believe its outpouring will be measured, rather than unchecked. He is a God of order, not chaos. There will not be one drop in the cup of His wrath that shouldn't be there. Our own wrath boils over in uncontrolled splatters. This is because our self-control is not absolute. His is. Possibly this, to Him, does not even feel like tension. We have no idea how skilled He is in compartmentalisation.

Two things arise out of this discourse. One, never make the mistake of thinking God *unfeeling*. And two, never forget that we are in fact talking about *our sin*. God has every right to be angry, frustrated, or wrathful over our sin. The fact that He holds it in check without any seeming effort is, frankly, a marvel.

For the first half of my life, I believed that God loved me mostly because He was contractually obliged to do so. 'Oh *bother*, I've written in My Word that I love people and will always be faithful to

My followers. This little [insert unflattering sobriquet] is really trying Me; but I suppose I should go on taking care of her, even though I'd really rather smack her upside the head.'

Nobody, I should note, has ever actually smacked me upside the head, though I metaphorically did it to myself all day long every day. My continual failure to live a life that was perfectly pure in every thought, word and deed haunted me. I spent my days blubbing apologies to God and spitting venom at myself. People told me I was too hard on myself, and I would respond that I was not nearly hard enough. Could they not see how pitiful my Christian performance was? How far from the ideal? That I was not giving the death of Jesus anything close to a decent return? And I tried *hard*. I could not understand those who apparently did not.

Coming into the concept of 'grace' in my mid-twenties was life-changing. Election for salvation *'does not, therefore, depend on human desire or effort, but on God's mercy.'* (Romans 9:16 NIV) 'No matter how hard you try to pay your way,' my mother said, 'it's never going to work, because it's not the right currency.' The resurgence in grace teaching in the '90s, conjoining with the movement recognising the daughters of the King as princesses, did a deep work in me. He did not see me as a recalcitrant brat, unable to make the grade, included in the Body by some unfortunate clerical error and bringing up the rear like the last staggering straggler in the 100m junior sprints. Instead, He saw me robed in gleaming white satin, spangled with gold: glowing, precious, treasured, full of sacred, secret potential and beauty. Crowned.

I would like to tell you that I never stumbled again, but this was just the beginning of my journey. It took a bit of therapy before I was ready to stop addressing myself with vitriol. One of the other keys to moving forward was finding out that the brain generates random thoughts as it bounces off stimuli, and that these did not actually

represent who I was as a person nor how poorly the work of Christ in me was progressing. You are not your worst thoughts unless you indulge them.

And God can't get enough of you. He pursues you, as He has pursued Israel and the nations, across time, through predestination and freewill, valleys of decision and bastions of stubbornness. He will never run out of patience because He cannot run out of who He is. But because He wants us to choose Him and His way freely … He has to live with the idea of patience sometimes going unrewarded.

It takes a long time to turn a life around, to get the heart facing the correction direction: 'further up and further in.' And so even the Lord understands a certain measure of what could be called 'failure'. No matter how hard He loves certain people, they will not turn. He tries strategy after strategy, plan after plan — not because He does not know the outcome, but because everything possible must be tried, and because Love cannot help itself but to keep trying. Right up 'til the very end, the Lord of all patience and active waiting will be offering us a rope. A bridge. A helicopter. A hand. His heart.

I once tearfully asked the Lord if I had derailed Plan A for my life. He laughed at me. 'Oh, child —' I imagined Him wiping His eyes '— we have a whole alphabet to work with!'

Inventors need patience while they are perfecting their inventions. But patience itself fosters invention in turn. God does

Patience drives invention as invention drives patience.

Princess

Your failures are all in the past
Do you worry that He sees you as you see yourself?
Your vision may be clouded in mist
But the day will come when your true reflection will tell:

Princess! He's calling your name
Princess! There is no call for shame
Daughter of the King, lift up your eyes
For the Prince of Peace is coming for His bride.

Sing aloud, Virgin Daughter of Zion
All has been restored, so stand a-glitter in gold
He loves you, o justified one
With a passion that shakes the heavens –
It's not something cold!

Princess! He's calling your name
Princess! There is no call for shame
Daughter of the King, lift up your eyes
For the Prince of Peace is coming for His bride ...

The beauty of holiness
Is given to the cherished one He chose.

not wait with arms folded, huffing and pointedly checking His watch. No. He works furiously, sleeves rolled up, to try to win you to Himself before your deadline. He is Himself a most tenacious lover.

We are not always falling over ourselves to dovetail into God's shaping processes. But He will never, ever give up on us.

I am convinced and confident of this very thing, that He who has begun a good work in you will [continue to] perfect and complete it until the day of Christ Jesus [the time of His return].

Philippians 1:6 AMP

Therefore ... let us throw off every encumbrance and the sin that so easily entangles, and let us run with endurance the race set out for us. Let us fix our eyes on Jesus, the author and perfecter of our faith ...

Hebrews 12:1b-2a BSB

By Their Fruit

O foolish Galatians! Who has bewitched you? It was before your eyes that Jesus Christ was publicly portrayed as crucified.

Galatians 3:1 ESV

THOSE FALSE PROPHETS AND TEACHERS Jesus warned about soon made themselves known. Most significant amongst them was a Jew educated in the Egyptian mysteries who became a thorn in the side of no less than three apostles – Peter, Paul and John. His name was Cerinthus and he taught that God was not the Creator of the world but that it had been made by a subsidiary authority, a malevolent demi-urge. Creation was therefore not good in essence, even if fallen in nature; rather it was corrupt from the start.

Cerinthus also claimed that Jesus was the biological son of Joseph and Mary and since, in his view, it was impossible for God to suffer, the 'Christ' spirit had descended on Jesus at His baptism but departed from Him before the crucifixion. Cerinthus further advocated that Gentile Christians should obey the Law of Moses and that males should be circumcised. He set up a school in the province of Galatia.

John the apostle is reported to have gone to the bathhouse in Ephesus. Spotting Cerinthus there, he rushed out, exclaiming, 'Let us fly, lest even the bathhouse fall down, because Cerinthus, the enemy of the truth, is inside!'

If it were not for Cerinthus, we probably wouldn't have the fourth gospel. John wrote it with the specific intention of countering the heretical doctrines spread by Cerinthus. It's also thought John's First and Second Epistles were written to provide corrections to these distortions of gospel teaching. Paul's letter to the Galatians was written to refute the changes Cerinthus was introducing and that were making such headway with new believers.

The Council of Jerusalem — described in Acts 15:1–35 — was convened after Paul and Barnabus were commissioned to get a ruling from the apostles once 'certain men' in Antioch disturbed the faith of believers by insisting Gentile Christians had to adhere to the Law of Moses. Those 'certain men' are believed to have been headed up by Cerinthus.

The Council decided on four basic rules for Gentiles that went back to an older law — that of Noah. They can be summarised as a single principle: Gentiles don't have to covenant with God according to the commands of the Torah, but they do have to refrain from any actions that would constitute a covenant with another deity.

No doubt when Paul returned to the mission field, he warned those who had been converted under his ministry about what Jesus had said regarding false teachers: they'll be known by their fruit.

And perhaps the Galatians sent back a message: *just what does that mean exactly? Could you define 'fruit' for us?*

Today, many ministries talk about 'good fruit' as if it means numerical growth, financial success, building expansion, donor engagement. It seems 'bad fruit' is negative publicity, dwindling attendance, curtailed spending. Conversations around 'fruit' tend to veer immediately towards recent attainments and achievements, not towards any increase in prayer or Bible study — thus telling us what's really valued by a ministry.

It's therefore fortunate for us that Paul set down just what the Fruit of the Spirit is, otherwise we'd be discerning it in worldly ways.

Patience is, of course, a key aspect of the Fruit because, being fruit, it doesn't spring up fully formed and in every way ripe and mature in an instant. It takes a season or two or three to grow. Paradoxically, patience is needed to grow patience. That immediately tells us it's only by grace that we can come into its fullness.

True patience is an ultra-fine balancing act. If it doesn't have an endpoint, then it's not patience at all. Rather, it's unwarranted passivity — as dangerous, if not more so, than impatience. Excessive patience is as ungodly as uncontrolled rage, since it can eventually lead to injustice, indifference, toleration of abuse and immense wasting.

Throughout Scripture, we see that, when the patience of God is interpreted as a licence for immorality, He calls a halt. His patience does not go on forever. Neither should ours. Yet it's always wise to ask the Spirit regarding the best time to draw it to a close.

Bad fruit

When it comes to picking out Galatians' antithesis of patience, we're truly spoiled for choice.

Immorality, in terms of premarital sex, is the opposite of patience because it says, 'Why wait?' and 'Why commit?' – among other things, of course. This is also true in terms of immoral gains. 'Why save up, when you can steal? Why work at a legitimate job when crime is so lucrative?'

Witchcraft is the opposite of patience because it tries to get a 'second opinion' and to manipulate circumstances when God is saying, 'Wait!' or 'No.'

Fits of rage are poles apart from patience because of their uncontrolled nature, lashing out when we don't immediately get our way. Delayed gratification is not considered; the fear of *no* gratification takes over, coupled with a complete lack of self-control or regard for others.

Envy opposes patience because it gets cranky that others have 'already' got more than we have. 'Why,' it asks, 'are *they* getting ahead, and I'm not?' Envy

---

Category 1:
Lustful things
sexual immorality
impurity
debauchery

Category 2:
Demonic things
idolatry
witchcraft

Category 3:
Divisive things
hatred
discord
jealousy
fits of rage
selfish ambition
dissensions
factions
envy

Category 4:
Unbridled things
fits of rage
drunkenness
orgies
and the like

not only accuses God of giving 'our entitlements' to others, but it fails to trust Him to give us what we need when He judges the time and need — to say nothing of our character — to be ripe.

Envy and immorality are close friends. They are both in the business of immediate satiation, regardless of whether circumstances are congenial, heedless of the other people impacted by their sin.

It's tempting to think envy is a lesser sin because it can, to some extent, be hidden in the heart. But here we are fooling ourselves on two counts.

One, you can't absolutely hide envy — not indefinitely. It will leak out. In my own life, it has flatulated out in barbed comments, passive aggressive behaviour, general defensiveness, sullen attitudes and emotional triggers. It is embarrassing to recall how poorly I have trusted the Lord, how ungrateful I have been. Because while others may have more, others may have less. And material blessings, opportunities, differing physicality — none of these things are the ultimate measure of blessedness.

We are blessed because we are loved and saved. Everything else is icing on top. We are welcome (even encouraged) to ask for more icing, but we are not welcome to accuse the Lord of caring less for us than He does for other people. How do we know what's inside their hearts? How do we know the role those blessings play, either in terms of compensation for past suffering, or in terms of resource underwriting for the Kingdom? How can we be sure that if we were to receive those blessings today, they would not become an idol in our lives? And what are we saying, subconsciously, about believers in the developing world? Do we somehow believe we *have* more because we *are* more? Is this not inconsistent and hypocritical?

Envy will, in the end, cause us to treat other people poorly. It is not a victimless crime at all. It will show up in our demeanour, our relationships, and in collegiate life. It will give us a sort of spiritual 'body odour' which turns people off even when they're not sure what, exactly, stinks.

Two, envy is not a lesser sin. It's the sin of unbelief, which is, if you'll pardon the parlance and the harshness, a hell-deserving offence. Ouch. It is also a sign of covetousness. Envy is not only a failure to trust God's discernment but also a failure to trust His love. We can disguise it as low self-esteem – 'I have less because I am less' – but there's no way we can mask the way it denigrates God's love. 'I am too icky to bless' is just a short step away from 'God is too picky to bless.'

This is the Universe-Maker who became a squally infant to grow up and die a horrible death in your place. Neither He nor you is deficient when it comes to loving you.

So trust Him. Trust that when it is your turn, it'll be your turn. Let Him continue to mould your character into the sort of person who can handle massive blessing without being distracted by it, dependent on it, or a hoarder of it. Rejoice with those who rejoice, and mourn with those who mourn. Be pure in your happiness for others' success. Borrow from the Lord's river of joy, if necessary, until yours is on tap.

There is another 'unpatience', not mentioned in our Galatians passage – *nōthroi,* an I've-given-up foot-dragging – which we've covered on page 69. Its foil is diligence: that which does not drop the ball over time, but continues to work with integrity toward the goal.

> Patience is not the ability to *wait* but the ability to *keep a good attitude* while waiting.
> —Joyce Meyer

Time & Iterations

One of the ways we see God demonstrating His patience is His willingness to work in phases and within the construct of time.

Creation could have been accomplished in an instant, in theory. A concept arises from the mind. When the mind is God's, the concept could appear fully formed. In fact, we have no proof that our God outside time did not, in fact, dream up, create, interact with, redeem, and transform the whole created order of time and space instantaneously! Even the word 'speed' is meaningless when we're talking about God. We have no idea how He might experience the invention we call 'time,' except that it is likely to be a voluntary option. We speak of 'eternity' and 'eternity past,' but that is from our point of view. To God, all may be a multi-dimensional Now. He walks and talks with us in real time, so He can certainly enter it. But He can also view it from the outside. And so King David and Jesus and every saint (capitalised or otherwise) can say:

> *I trust in You, O L*ORD*;*
> *I say, 'You are my God.'*
> *My times are in Your hands …*

Psalm 31:14–15a BSB

> *You saw me before I was born.*
> *Every day of my life was recorded in Your book.*
> *Every moment was laid out*
> *before a single day had passed.*

Psalm 139:16 NLT

'*All the days ordained for me,*' the NIV puts it!

The Lord of the fourth dimension is not subject to it. He is not obligated to preserve or enshrine the past. He is able to voluntarily forget our sins, though there is nothing wrong with His memory. He is both the Ancient of Days and a young Lamb. So when He says in Revelation 21: 21:5-6a NIV,

> 'I am making everything new!' Then He said, 'Write this down, for these words are trustworthy and true.' He said to me: 'It is done. I am the Alpha and the Omega, the Beginning and the End.'

... He is letting us know that since He Himself IS both ends of the spectrum, He holds the rights to everything on it.

Why did He choose to invent 'days' and then take six of them to complete the Earth? We don't know. It could be as simple as 'it was more fun that way.' Admit it — Lego is fun no matter how old you are. And the fun of making something all in one go is not the same fun as adding to a project a little at a time. The funnest projects of all are the renovations.

And so, first we get Eden and then Jerusalem and then Yahweh-Shammah. In Exodus 14 He shows us how He can part the sea and lead us into the desert; in Isaiah 40 He sends someone *out of* the desert and rearranges the landscape completely.

In Isaiah 43 NIV, God reminds Israel that even though it seems to carry little practical weight with them, His track record is not all there is to Him.

While the Lord references the Exodus from Egypt, this passage is on the heels of the previous chapter where the coming Spirit-filled Servant to the Gentiles is described very differently:

> *... a smoldering wick He will not snuff out ...*
> *til He establishes justice in the earth ...*

Isaiah 43:15-21

'I am the LORD, your Holy One,
Israel's Creator, your King.'

This is what the LORD says —
He who made a way through the sea,
a path through the mighty waters,
who drew out the chariots and horses,
the army and reinforcements together,
and they lay there, never to rise again,
extinguished, snuffed out like a wick:

'Forget the former things;
do not dwell on the past.
See, I am doing a new thing!
Now it springs up; do you not perceive it?
I am making a way in the wilderness
and streams in the wasteland.
The hayyat [living creature/horde] honour Me,
the tannim [dragons] and the ya'anah [vampire spirit],
because I provide water in the wilderness
and streams in the wasteland,
to give drink to My people, My chosen,
the people I formed for Myself
that they may proclaim My praise.'

God declares a day when the past and present are overturned into what they should be. The only constant is He Himself who was, and is, and is to come.

Sometimes I like to indulge in a little time-travelling daydream. But for all the technological showing off, I always come up against two things that would be awkward to reveal to historical people. One is the swings-and-roundabouts gains and losses. For instance, women can do anything now and be taken seriously, compassionate respect is valued, and the Word of God is freely available most places; but society has largely discarded belief and clean living to a degree that would shock our forebears. And the other is the devastating fact that even as late as the year I'm daydreaming in, the Lord has not yet returned.

It is hard to be patient about the Second Coming when the world continues to go down the tubes in many ways, even whilst advancing beautifully in other respects. 'Come, Lord Jesus!' our hearts cry. And yet, this is our golden, last-ditch opportunity. To occupy. To steward the planet as we were called to do. To be the groundswell of the growing, eventual Kingdom that fills the Earth. To be the early adopters of the winning side, to help save the precious lost while we still can – to play a part in amassing the mulititude from every tribe and tongue, language and nation. To train as kings and priests, not in an environment which privileges that, but in enemy-occupied territory. To be Narnian while still obliged to live at Experiment House. To be the Logres.

> *Be patient [makrothymēsate], therefore, brothers, until the coming of the Lord. See how the farmer waits [ekdechetai] for the precious fruit of the earth, being patient [makrothymōn] about it, until it receives the early*

and the late rains. You also, be patient. **Establish** *your hearts, for the coming of the Lord is at hand.*

sterixate — strengthen, establish, set fast, to turn resolutely in a certain direction, to confirm

James 5:7–8 ESV

Is it our fault that He has not yet returned? The gospel must be preached in every corner. If we have not given that task traction, perhaps we are delaying Him. He is not willing for anyone to perish, although He knows many will. He will hold out His hand until the very last second. Even in His justified wrath there will be the sorrow of having to watch His beloved, stubborn, hair-numbered children passing from existence. He will never regret the annihilation of their sin. But He will not enjoy their clinging to it as it burns. We should be as dedicated to saving them as He is — for this is what He lived and died for, what He waits and holds back for.

End-Times Endurance

At the risk of hypothesising above my pay grade, I would like to take a ridiculously shallow dive into the ocean of eschatology: the study of the End Times.

Revelation 13:10 NIV warns of dire events that will call for *'patient endurance* [hypomonē] *and faithfulness* [pistis] *on the part of God's people.'* Revelation 14:12 NIV reiterates, *'This calls for patient endurance* [hypomonē] *on the part of the people of God who keep His commands and remain faithful* [pistin] *to Jesus.'* So ... what are these events, and who are the Christians referred to?

One of the challenges with Revelation is that there's no guarantee that what John saw, or wrote, was linear, let alone how much was allegorical. We're not even told if they're an array of various alternate futures, all of them resulting in God winning. Some of the book is

clearly 'macro' – panoscopic metaphor – and some could even belong to the deep past. Each section of the vision could overlap or circle back to another. Even when John says, 'Then I saw,' we don't know if he was *shown* the 'next' thing; we only know it was what he *saw* next. So, when it comes to a coherent timeline, we can only guess; that's why there is so much difference of opinion in the field. Daniel, Isaiah, Ezekiel, Zechariah, 1 Corinthians and 2 Thessalonians are all in the mix. All of the following discussion, therefore, is speculation based on what *could* be a sequence of events. I'm not wedded to it, and you are under no obligation to agree with it.

Some eschatology teaches that the Rapture – when all the believers are caught up to meet the Lord in the air – happens before the Great Tribulation (because we are not appointed to suffer wrath). Others are sure that it will happen after or during the Tribulation (because believers of some stripe do get killed in it).

Of the 'holy people' on Earth during that time, we can't tell for sure if they are Jews, if they are us (we who currently believe), or if they are people (marked or unmarked) who come to their senses after we're gone. (That's *if* we are gone; just because we are caught up into the air and changed in the twinkling of an eye, doesn't mean we don't float back down again. Zechariah 9:16 BSB sounds suspiciously like the transformed saints ruling and reigning: *'On that day the Lord their God will save them as the flock of His people; for like jewels in a crown they will sparkle over His land.'*)

Again, what we are looking for is an explanation of why the faithful need endurance, and *if* we ourselves are all gone by the time of the Tribulation, who 'the faithful' might then be.

Overleaf, I have humbly attempted to diagram these events as they appear to me. As I said, it's hard to know if they are the same scene told from different angles, consequent scenes, or a scattering of scenes. Take it all with a grain of salt. In the final analysis, whoever *is* around for these events will need patient endurance because life will not be pretty. In addition, if we ever come to love the lost like God does, seeing them suffer His wrath will be as hard for us as it is for Him. We know we are sinners saved by grace. There will be no room for gloating — only for desperate thankfulness.

Tribulation isn't just an end-of-the-world scenario. It's been going on, variously scaled, since the inception of the Church. Around 56AD, Paul wrote Romans 8:18–28 NIV:

> I consider that our present sufferings are not worth comparing with the glory that will be revealed in us. For the creation **waits** in **eager expectation** for the children of God to be revealed. For the creation was subjected to **frustration**, not by its own choice, but by the will of the one who subjected it, in hope that the creation itself will be liberated from its bondage to decay and brought into the freedom and glory of the children of God.

apekdechomai — to expect fully

apokaradokia — intense anticipation

mataiotes — uselessness, depravity, transientness

Right at the beginning, Paul was thinking about the end. Creation — the whole created order — longs for us to come into our inheritance in God, and take it with us. And so we will receive a new Heaven (or heavens) and a new Earth. And while we wait and suffer, as the universe waits and suffers, we can look forward to a glory that is orders of magnitude above our suffering. It's a price tag that's a total bargain, though I'm sure it won't feel like it at the time.

Interestingly, though it's easy to read this as 'we will live in an environment of glory,' it actually says the reverse: that the glory will be something *within* us. *We ourselves* will be the environment of glory in which the world participates. We will be New Humans, kings and priests, ruling and reigning with Christ. What does a king do? Administration and inspiration. What does a priest do? Connects and reconciles people with God.

Revelation 7
On Earth: 144,000 Israelis are sealed.
In Heaven before the Lamb's throne:
a multinational multitude of saints
from the Tribulation, worshipping.

Israel & the church?

Revelation 11
The two witnesses are killed,
and after half a 'week'
they go up to Heaven in a cloud.

Revelation 12
The satan-dragon loses the heavenly war
and is kicked out of court for good.
He goes to wage war against the faithful.

humanity?

Revelation 13
The **supernatural** dragon allies with the **sea** beast
and conquers the holy: Israel/the church.
This beast is given authority over all people,
and all people worship it,
except those whose names are in the Book.
The **land** produces a third beast ally,
as if completing a counterfeit trinity.
This beast forces the mark, and has a number.

Revelation 14
The Lamb stands on Mt Zion with
144,000 blameless 'firstfruit' Israelis,
bearing His own seal and singing.
An angel takes over evangelism of the earth,
and warns that mark-receivers will drink the
wrath of God and suffer torment without respite.

When are the names written? At surrender, or at predestination?
If the Lamb is slain from the foundation of the Earth,
then possibly the names are all written in the Book of Life then.
This means that there are people on earth refusing to worship the beast,
and not yet worshipping the Lord, but called to do so.
It also means that there are worshippers during this time
who are vulnerable to captivity and execution.
And **this** is what they need to be patient about.

The idea of 'firstfruits' could indicate that they are a tithe
representing the rest of the holy (the Church).
It's not clear if we ourselves are with them or not.
If we are, then there are no believers left on earth
at this stage – only those who have not yet repented.

This is where I think it possible that mark-bearers
can repent and be saved, though by then it's too late to escape
the wrath on earth if 'that ship has sailed' with the Rapture.
And **that** would be why the next words are,
'You new saints will need patient endurance, and will be blessed
if you die in the Lord from now on, and gain rest.'

The Word continues:

> We know that the whole creation has been groaning as in the pains of childbirth right up to the present time. Not only so, but we ourselves, who have the firstfruits of the Spirit, groan inwardly as we **wait eagerly** for our adoption to sonship, the redemption of our bodies. For in this hope we were saved. But hope that is seen is no hope at all. Who hopes for what they already have? But if we hope for what we do not yet have, we **wait for it patiently**.

apekdechomenoi — rather like *qavah*

hypomonēs apekdechometha — in patience we await eagerly

This is our task: to bear the strain between the *now* and the *not yet*. To trust Him in a spirit of joyful anticipation and press on toward the mark. Our longing is not tinged with despair or grief, but with hope. The Spirit Himself feels this tension with our progress, and gets involved:

> In the same way, the Spirit helps us in our weakness. We do not know what we ought to pray for, but the Spirit Himself intercedes for us through wordless groans. And He who searches our hearts knows the mind of the Spirit, because the Spirit intercedes for God's people in accordance with the will of God.

> And we know that in all things God works for the good of those who love Him, who have been called according to His purpose. For those God foreknew He also predestined to be conformed to the image of His Son, that He might be the firstborn among many brothers and sisters. And those He predestined, He also called; those He called, He also justified; those He justified, He also glorified.

As they say in the country of my birth:

> *Kia kaha, kia māia, kia manawanui.*
> Be strong. Be steadfast. Be willing.

Finally, be strong in the Lord and in His mighty power. Put on the full armour of God, so that you can take your stand against the devil's schemes.

Ephesians 6:10–11 BSB

*I will stand at my guard post
and station myself on the ramparts.*
I will watch to see what He will say to me,
*and how I should answer when corrected.
Then the LORD answered me:
'Write down this vision
and clearly inscribe it on tablets,
so that a herald may run with it.*
For the vision awaits an appointed time;
it testifies of the end and does not lie.
Though it lingers, wait [chakah] **for it,**
*since it will surely come
and will not delay.'*

Habakkuk 2:1–3
BSB

From the

I LOVE WRITING CHILDREN'S BOOKS — I've written several. Drawing up from the deep wellspring inside, I repeatedly find that the statement of George MacDonald, a nineteenth century writer who so deeply inspired CS Lewis is absolutely accurate: 'A man may well himself discover truth in what he wrote; for he was dealing all the time with things that came from thoughts beyond his own.'

Now writing novels is much more difficult than non-fiction. Structure matters. So I've studied far more about writing fiction for teens than I have on any other aspect of the novel. Anyone involved in such intensive study is inevitably brought face-to-face with the philosophic bent of the most popular modern writers for young adults. One very famous Australian writer said about the darkness in his novels: 'Why should I give young people hope when there is no hope for them?'

Back in the last decade of last century, a study commissioned by the main local newspaper in my city uncovered the fact that in 85% of the books for teens available at that time and printed in the previous ten years the protagonist had either committed suicide or contemplated it. The darkness in such novels is so pervasive and so expected that a long fantasy I wrote for teens and tweens was, despite winning an award, classified as a middle-grade reader for no other reason than that the story ended happily.

Now although most authors for teens would be reluctant to admit it, their viewpoints

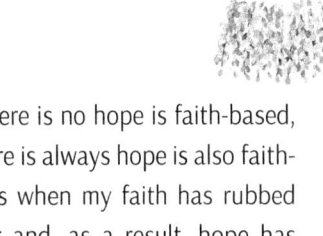

are religious ones. The idea that there is no hope is faith-based, just as my alternative view that there is always hope is also faith-based. Now there have been times when my faith has rubbed away to an incredibly thin veneer and, as a result, hope has waned to almost nothing. However, it never dropped to zero and stayed there.

One of the most significant questions we can ask our hearts is this: 'Do I actually believe in the fairytale ending? The happily-ever-after that comes after many trials?' The story of Christianity is the most wondrous of all eucatastrophes—Tolkien's word meaning *good catastrophe*, a sudden unexpected turn of events where unavoidable disaster is averted and all is well and not only that but, as Julian of Norwich said, all shall be well and all manner of things shall be well.

Unless we retain a crumb of faith, a mustard-seed's worth, that God will indeed come through for us and that it's genuinely true all shall be well, then we simply can't keep on hoping. We only need a tiny amount of faith—just enough to persuade us to reach for Jesus. He's the one whose faith does the real heavy lifting: we only need enough to take the hand He's already holding out to us.

Without faith, the fruit of patience will not be able to mature in our lives. Without hope, we will jettison faith. And the bottom line, as a consequence, is that the spirit of wasting which is overcome by the fruit of patience cannot be removed from our lives.

So wisdom tells us to ask God to restore our belief in a happily-ever-after and to bring back hope.

When the people of Israel were at Mount Sinai, God pledged that – if they obeyed – He would send an angel ahead of them into the Promised Land to drive out their enemies. But they had to be patient because the angel would work slowly:

> But I will not drive them out in a single year, because the land would become desolate and the wild animals too numerous for you. Little by little I will drive them out

before you, until you have increased enough to take possession of the land.

Exodus 23:29–30 NIV

Here God reveals that we need patience in particular situations because, if the circumstances were remedied too quickly, a power void would result. Wildness — chaos and confusion — would ensue. All our advances would be wasted, if the land could not be occupied, fortified and held. Often we'd like God to intervene in our lives but, if He did too spectacularly, we'd be unable to maintain our gains. So He works slowly, with deep patience, so our gains are not lost.

PLACES TO START

Tribulation offers us a chance to level up in patience. Concentrate on Jesus. Using your own words in the way you are accustomed to relating to Him, a prayer similar to this one may help.

Lord, we both know that patience is hard to develop. And even though You are supremely trustworthy, there are times I fail to trust Your timing. I'm sorry for the insult this represents. You are good — all the time — and You do not change like shifting shadows.

Lord, I want to thank You for the immense patience You have shown to the human race. For so long, we — myself included — have held out on You and turned our faces away from You. This was wrong.

Thank You also for the way You have been patient and forgiving and faithful to me, personally. It's taking me a long time to conform to Your magnificent image, Lord, so I'm very grateful that You're here for the long haul. You promise to never give up on me.

Lord, please help me to display and develop Your patience with the world and the people around me. Help me to know when to act and when to refrain, when to sit back and trust You and when to step out in faith. Help me develop a passionate readiness while Your purposes coalesce. Let me be entwined with You every minute. May I represent You better and better as I lean on Your enabling grace in our walk together. I submit my soul to You in hope, in trust, in confidence that You will finish what You've started in me.

With all my heart, mind, soul and strength,
in the name of my Saviour Jesus of Nazareth,
Amen.

> *May the God of endurance and encouragement grant you to live in such harmony with one another, in accord with Christ Jesus, that together you may with one voice glorify the God and Father of our Lord Jesus Christ.*
>
> Romans 15:5–6
> ESV

Aligning Three

Galatians 5:13–15
New International Version

Galatians 5:13–15
The Message

*You, my brothers and sisters, were called to be **free**. But do not use your freedom to indulge the **flesh**; rather, serve one another humbly in love.*

It is absolutely clear that God has called you to a free life. Just make sure that you don't use this freedom as an excuse to do whatever you want to do and destroy your freedom. Rather, use your freedom to serve one another in love; that's how freedom grows.

*For the entire law is fulfilled in keeping this one command: 'Love your neighbour as yourself.' If you **bite** and **devour** each other, watch out or you will be **destroyed** by each other.*

For everything we know about God's Word is summed up in a single sentence: Love others as you love yourself. That's an act of true freedom. If you bite and ravage each other, watch out — in no time at all you will be annihilating each other, and where will your precious freedom be then?

Modern Versions

| Galatians 5:13–15 The Passion Translation | Notes STRONG'S |

Beloved ones, God has called us to live a life of freedom in the Holy Spirit. But don't view this wonderful freedom as an opportunity to set up a base of operations in the natural realm. Freedom means that we become so completely free of self-indulgence that we become servants of one another, expressing love in all we do.

For love completes the laws of God. All of the law can be summarized in one grand statement:
  'Demonstrate love to your neighbor, even as you care for and love yourself.'
But if you continue to criticize and come against each other over minor issues, you're acting like wild beasts trying to destroy one another!

eleutheria
freedom (especially from slavery), liberty

sarx
sinful human state

katesthiete
eat all up, devour, squander, annoy, injure

darknete
bite, backbite, harm seriously, thwart

analothete
use up, destroy

Galatians 5:16–18
NIV

Galatians 5:16–18
MSG

*So I say, **walk** by the Spirit, and you will not gratify the desires of the flesh. For the flesh desires what is contrary to the Spirit, and the Spirit what is contrary to the flesh. They are in conflict with each other, so that you are not to do whatever you want. But if you are led by the Spirit, you are not under the law.*

My counsel is this: Live freely, animated and motivated by God's Spirit. Then you won't feed the compulsions of selfishness. For there is a root of sinful self-interest in us that is at odds with a free spirit, just as the free spirit is incompatible with selfishness. These two ways of life are antithetical, so that you cannot live at times one way and at times another way according to how you feel on any given day. Why don't you choose to be led by the Spirit and so escape the erratic compulsions of a law-dominated existence?

Galatians 5:16–18
TPT

Notes
STRONG'S

As you yield freely and fully to the dynamic life and power of the Holy Spirit, you will abandon the cravings of your self-life. For your self-life craves the things that offend the Holy Spirit and hinder him from living free within you! And the Holy Spirit's intense cravings hinder your old self-life from dominating you! So then, the two incompatible and conflicting forces within you are your self-life of the flesh and the new creation life of the Spirit.

But when you are brought into the full freedom of the Spirit of grace, you will no longer be living under the domination of the law, but soaring above it!

peripateo
live, deport, follow

Galatians 5:19–21
NIV

Galatians 5:19–21
MSG

The acts of the flesh are obvious: **sexual immorality, impurity** *and* **debauchery; idolatry** *and* **witchcraft; hatred, discord, jealousy, fits of rage, selfish ambition, dissensions, factions** *and* **envy; drunkenness, orgies,** *and the like.*

It is obvious what kind of life develops out of trying to get your own way all the time: repetitive, loveless, cheap sex; a stinking accumulation of mental and emotional garbage; frenzied and joyless grabs for happiness; trinket gods; magic-show religion; paranoid loneliness; cutthroat competition; all-consuming-yet-never-satisfied wants; a brutal temper; an impotence to love or be loved; divided homes and divided lives; small-minded and lopsided pursuits; the vicious habit of depersonalizing everyone into a rival; uncontrolled and uncontrollable addictions; ugly parodies of community. I could go on.

I warn you, as I did before, that those who live like this will not inherit the kingdom of God.

This isn't the first time I have warned you, you know. If you use your freedom this way, you will not inherit God's kingdom.

Galatians 5:19–21
TPT

Notes
STRONG'S

The cravings of the self-life are obvious: Sexual immorality, lustful thoughts, pornography, chasing after things instead of God, manipulating others, hatred of those who get in your way, senseless arguments, resentment when others are favored, temper tantrums, angry quarrels, only thinking of yourself, being in love with your own opinions, being envious of the blessings of others, murder, uncontrolled addictions, wild parties, and all other similar behavior.

Haven't I already warned you that those who use their "freedom" for these things will not inherit the kingdom realm of God!

porneia — harlotry
akatharsia — uncleanness
aselgeia — lasciviousness
eidolatreia — image-worship
pharmakeia — sorcery
echthrai — hostility, enmity
eris — discord, strife
zelos — envy
thumos — fierceness, wrath
eritheia — conspiracy, intrigue
dichostis — disunion, sedition
hairesis — choice (of a sect)
pthonos — jealousy, spite
methe — drunkenness
komos — carousing, rioting

Galatians 5:22–24
NIV

Galatians 5:22–24
MSG

*But the fruit of the Spirit is **love, joy, peace, forbearance, kindness, goodness, faithfulness, gentleness** and **self-control.***

But what happens when we live God's way? He brings gifts into our lives, much the same way that fruit appears in an orchard — things like affection for others, exuberance about life, serenity. We develop a willingness to stick with things, a sense of compassion in the heart, and a conviction that a basic holiness permeates things and people. We find ourselves involved in loyal commitments, not needing to force our way in life, able to marshal and direct our energies wisely.

Against such things there is no law. Those who belong to Christ Jesus have crucified the flesh with its passions and desires.

Legalism is helpless in bringing this about; it only gets in the way. Among those who belong to Christ, everything connected with getting our own way and mindlessly responding to what everyone else calls necessities is killed off for good — crucified.

 Galatians 5:22–24 TPT

 Notes STRONG'S

But the fruit produced by the Holy Spirit within you is divine love in all its varied expressions:

agape — unconditional love

*joy that overflows,
peace that subdues,
patience that endures,
kindness in action,
a life full of virtue,
faith that prevails,
gentleness of heart, and
strength of spirit.*

chara — joy

eirene — peace

makrothumia — patience

chrestotes — kindness

agathosune — goodness

Never set the law above these qualities, for they are meant to be limitless.

pistis — faith, fidelity

Keep in mind that we who belong to Jesus, the Anointed One, have already experienced crucifixion. For everything connected with our self-life was put to death on the cross and crucified with Messiah.

prautes — gentleness, humility

egkrateia — self control

Galatians 5:25–26
NIV

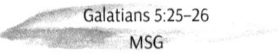
Galatians 5:25–26
MSG

*Since we live by the Spirit, let us **keep in step** with the Spirit. Let us not become **conceited**, provoking and envying each other.*

Since this is the kind of life we have chosen, the life of the Spirit, let us make sure that we do not just hold it as an idea in our heads or a sentiment in our hearts, but work out its implications in every detail of our lives. That means we will not compare ourselves with each other as if one of us were better and another worse. We have far more interesting things to do with our lives. Each of us is an original.

Galatians 5:25–26
TPT

Notes
STRONG'S

We must live in the Holy Spirit and follow after Him. So may we never be arrogant, or look down on another, for each of us is an original. We must forsake all jealousy that diminishes the value of others.

stoicheo
to march in lockstep

kenodoxos
vainglorious

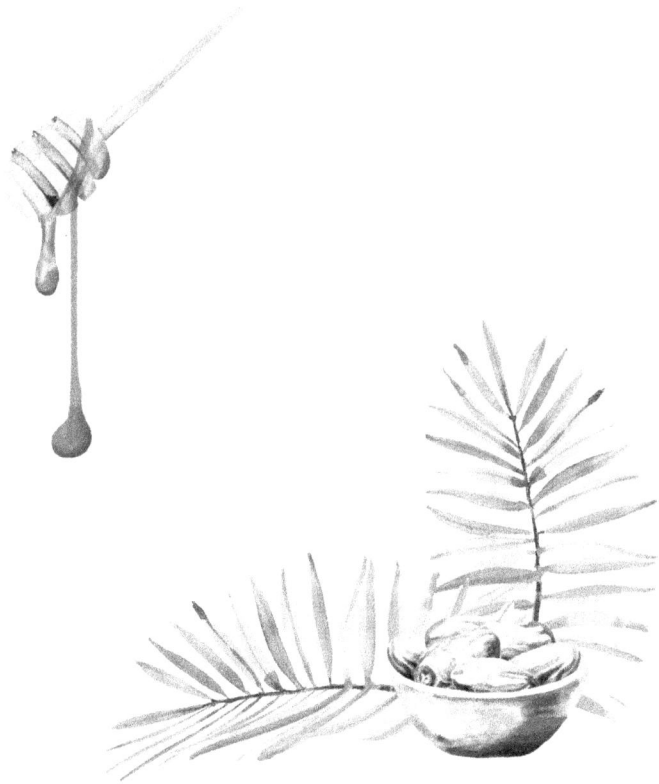

References

Holy Bible

Biblica, www.biblegateway.com

www.biblehub.com

Amplified Bible, Classic Edition (AMPC) © 1954, 1958, 1962, 1964, 1965, 1987 by The Lockman Foundation

Berean Study Bible (BSB) and Berean Literal Bible (BLB) Copyright ©2016 by Bible Hub. Used by Permission. All Rights Reserved Worldwide.

Christian Standard Bible (CSB) Copyright © 2017 by Holman Bible Publishers. Used by permission. Christian Standard Bible®, and CSB® are federally registered trademarks of Holman Bible Publishers, all rights reserved.

Complete Jewish Bible (CJB) Copyright © 1998 by David H. Stern. All rights reserved.

English Standard Version® (ESV). Copyright © 2001 by Crossway, a publishing ministry of Good News Publishers. Used by permission. All rights reserved.

GOD'S WORD Translation (GW) All Scripture marked with the designation "GW" is taken from GOD'S WORD®. © 1995, 2003, 2013, 2014, 2019, 2020 by God's Word to the Nations Mission Society. Used by permission.

King James Version of the Bible (KJV). Public domain.

Literal Standard Version (LSV) Copyright © 2020 Covenant Press and the Covenant Christian Coalition. Creative Commons.

Legacy Standard Bible®,(LSB), Copyright © 2021 by The Lockman Foundation. Used by permission. All rights reserved. Managed in partnership with Three Sixteen Publishing Inc. LSBible.org and 316publishing.com.

New American Bible, revised edition (NAB) © 2010, 1991, 1986, 1970 Confraternity of Christian Doctrine, Washington, D.C. and are used by permission of the copyright owner. All Rights Reserved.

New American Standard Bible® (NASB). Copyright © 1960, 1962, 1963, 1968, 1971, 1972, 1973, 1975, 1977, 1995 by The Lockman Foundation. Used by permission. (www.Lockman.org)

A New English Translation of the Septuagint, ©2007 by the International Organization for Septuagint and Cognate Studies, Inc. All rights reserved.

New International Version® (NIV®). Copyright © 1973, 1978, 1984, 2011 by Biblica, Inc.™ Used by permission of Zondervan. All rights reserved worldwide. www.zondervan.com The "NIV" and "New International Version" are trademarks registered in the United States Patent and Trademark Office by Biblica, Inc.™.

New King James Version (NKJV). Copyright © 1982 by Thomas Nelson, Inc. Used by permission. All rights reserved.

New Living Translation (NLT). Copyright 1996, 2004. Used by permission of Tyndale House Publishers, Inc., Wheaton, Illinois 60189. All rights reserved.

New Revised Standard Version of the Bible (NRS). Copyright 1952 [2nd edition, 1971] by the Division of Christian Education of the National Council of the Churches of Christ in the United States of America. Used by permission. All rights reserved.

The Message (MSG). Copyright © 1993, 2002, 2018 by Eugene H. Peterson

The Passion Translation® (TPT). Copyright © 2017,2018 by Passion & Fire Ministries, Inc. Used by permission. All rights reserved. ThePassionTranslation.com.

The Voice Copyright ©2011 Thomas Nelson, Inc. The Voice™ translation © 2011 Ecclesia Bible Society. All rights reserved.

World English Bible (WEB). Public Domain.

Ellis, Paul: **Letters From Jesus: Finding Good News in Christ's Letters to the Churches.** KingsPress, 2019
Foxe, John: **Actes and Monuments (Foxe's Book of Martyrs).** John Day, 1563
Hamilton, Anne: **Dealing with Rachab: Spirit of Wasting.** Armour Books, 2025
Hardon, John: **Catholic Dictionary: An Abridged and Updated Edition of Modern Catholic Dictionary.** Christian/Forum, 2014
Ignatius, of Loyola, Saint, 1491-1556. **The Spiritual Exercises of St. Ignatius Loyola: a New Translation by Elisabeth Meier Tetlow.** Lanham, MD: University Press of America, 1987.
Jersak, Brad: **The Gospel in Chairs.** www.youtube.com/watch?v=N7FKhHScgUQ
Julian of Norwich: **Revelations of Divine Love.** Translation: Clifton Wolters, Penguin, 1966
Lewis, C.S.: **That Hideous Strength: A Modern Fairy-Tale for Grown-Ups.** The Bodley Head, 1945
Lewis, C.S.: **The Silver Chair.** The Bodley Head, 1953
Lewis, C.S.: **The Last Battle.** The Bodley Head, 1956
NAS Exhaustive Concordance of the Bible with Hebrew-Aramaic and Greek Dictionaries Copyright © 1981, 1998 by The Lockman Foundation Copyright © 2021 by Discovery Bible.
Nietzsche, Friedrich: **Beyond Good and Evil: Prelude to a Philosophy of the Future.** C.G. Naumann, 1886
Peterson, Eugene: **A Long Obedience in the Same Direction: Discipleship in an Instant Society.** InterVarsity Press, 1980
Robinson, Rebekah: *Princess.* Day in the Sun, Aisle 6 Records, 2006
Robinson, Rebekah: **Someone to Look Up To.** Beckon Creative, 2019
Robinson, Rebekah & Hamilton, Anne: **Core Values: Love.** Beckon Creative, 2022
Robinson, Rebekah & Hamilton, Anne: **Core Values: Joy.** Beckon Creative, 2023
Robinson, Rebekah & Hamilton, Anne: **Core Values: Peace.** Beckon Creative, 2024
Sandford, Mark: **Turning the Hearts of Fathers.** Armour Books, 2022
Strong, J.: **The New Strong's Expanded Exhaustive Concordance of the Bible.** Nashville: Thomas Nelson, 2010

www.webmd.com/diet/medjool-dates-health-benefits, 2 August 2023
www.britannica.com/plant/date-palm, 4 May 2024
https://biblehub.com/greek/1690.htm, 27 January 2025
www.bibletools.org/index.cfm/fuseaction/Lexicon.show/ID/G5278, 24 July 2024
www.etymonline.com/search?q=patient, 26 January 2025
www.pres-outlook.org/2021/05/patience-the-longsuffering-fruit-of-the-spirit, 11 May 2022
www.sefaria.org/sheets/415572?lang=bi, 27 January 2025
https://www.healthline.com/nutrition/benefits-of-dates#TOC_TITLE_HDR_7, 27 January 2025
www. hebrew.jerusalemprayerteam.org/patience, 27 January 2025

The quotation of certain works is not intended as a wholesale endorsement of that author or work.

Spider web: Things that have remained in one place for some time often attract spider webs. There's something about a webbed object that says, 'Waiting …!'

Dates make a good motif for *patience* for several reasons. Because the B vitamins in dates fight fatigue, they encourage stamina and perseverance. Date palms take 10–15 years to reach full fruiting maturity. A single branch can take some time to harvest, as it may bear more than a thousand dates! The English fruit name 'date' comes from Greek *daktulos*, 'finger.'

There are more than 600 varieties of dates. Patience and its coping mechanisms are as varied as we are! Dates are high in antioxidants, fibre and nutrients. Preliminary studies show that they may aid brain and bone health, childbirth, and glucose balance.

As a linguistic coincidence, patience itself must often range over many, many *calendar dates* or *digits!* This English time-word 'date' comes from Latin *data epistola,* 'a letter given or received at a particular time,' originating from *dare,* 'to give.' This is the day – even when it's a day of waiting – that the Lord has made. It's a gift; that's why, as the quip goes, it's called *the present*. All the days ordained for us are written in His book, Psalm 139:16 tells us. A big bunch of ripening dates.

Dates were one of the Seven Species of the Promised Land (featured on the covers of this series) which were counted as acceptable Firstfruits offerings.

It's a land of wheat and barley, of vines and fig trees and pomegranates, a land of oil-rich olive trees and date honey. In that land, you'll always have plenty to eat – you won't lack anything!

Deuteronomy 8:8–9 VOICE

Warrior: The soldier represents the military history of the Galatians.

Lavender: As it is planted in rows, it speaks of the Galatian cadres' military discipline and marching in lockstep.

Notes

When the Bible speaks of the Promised Land in terms of 'a land flowing with milk and honey,' this is **date honey**, or date syrup. While bees were kept in Israel, and certainly honeycomb is mentioned, date honey was apparently more common. A land flowing in milk (pasturelands for dairy animals) and honey (plentiful date palms) is a picture of bucolic potential and – to a people lost in sand and scrub for four decades, living on manna – beauty and bounty. Grape bunches the size of cows didn't hurt, either!

Date syrup (available at the supermarket) is a reduction of boiled, mashed dates, similar to golden syrup treacle but much darker, far more nutritious, and possessing a wonderful exotic flavour.

The DNA of God Series

Titles in the works!

DEALING WITH RACHAB:
Spirit of Wasting

ISBN 978-1-925380-87-3

The spirit of wasting is not hard to overcome if you've first mastered the spirit of rejection. However, she's not going to take defeat quietly, so she marshals the other threshold guardians in a combined assault. Their primary agenda is to ensure we're tied up in an unbreakable double bind.

As we examine Scripture, we'll note that the doulbe binds mentioned there always involve denial of access to the atonement. We can't lose our salvation, but we can lose some of its temporal benefits. Even Jesus didn't find dismantling such double binds easy, but He provides us with a way forward.

DEALING WITH AZAZEL:
Spirit of Rejection

ISBN 978-1-9253802-9-3

'I am your only friend.' That's the playbook line that works so superbly for the spirit of rejection. Most of us fall for it without even realising that our coping mechanisms—fight, flight, freeze, flatter, forestall or forget—are actually undermining our every effort to overcome this entity. What exactly can we do to subdue the spirit of rejection in our lives without sabotaging ourselves in the process?

This is the seventh book in the series, *Strategies for the Threshold*, and is the most highly anticipated volume so far. It addresses the nature of the spirit and also references to it in Scripture, its wider agenda, its spiritual legal rights, and its propensity for following after you to undo the good that you do.

HIDDEN IN THE CLEFT:
True and False Refuge

ISBN 978-1-9253801-4-9

Jesus had a refuge – a safe haven – He retreated to when His life was in danger.

What does His choice reveal about where best to find sanctuary in times of trouble? What is the significance of the hiding place He used for an entire season? How can we discern the difference between a true and false refuge?

Removal of our false refuges is the first step towards achieving our life's calling-- the divine purpose for which God created us. Yet all too often we fail to recognise how we've defaulted to a false refuge when disappointment strikes.

This book offers practical help, hope and encouragement towards achieving your destiny in Christ.

DEALING WITH KRONOS:
Spirit of Abuse and Time

ISBN 978-1-9253804-9-1

The oldest stories about 'Father Time' describe an entity with a seraph's body, and heads like the angelic cherubim. Kronos is a voracious spirit of abuse who consumes the past. Bound in chains to prevent him eating the future, nevertheless through the power of unresolved past trauma he wants to devour the present too.

We can believe we've escaped abuse when, in reality, complicity with Kronos has locked us into a maximum security spiritual prison. We need the Redeemer of wasted time to aid us. Scripture provides unexpected and important principles for dealing with the tactics, agenda and ploys of Kronos.

This book is a companion volume to *Dealing with Belial*.

GOD'S PAGEANTRY:
The Threshold Guardians & the Covenant Defender

ISBN 978-0-9803620-7-7

Constriction. Wasting. Recognise them? Met them just as the door opened into your calling? Found that not only were events conspiring against you but you were self-sabotaging? Lost your faith and felt betrayed when your dreams fell in on you?

A critical loss of knowledge about the existence and nature of threshold/ cornerstone covenants has occurred in the last century. We no longer have any idea how perilous or complex spiritual doorways are. Many of us put ourselves in harm's way and abandon hope we'll ever step into our destinies.

GOD'S PAGEANTRY is about the obstacles we encounter, the covenants we face and the armour we need to pass over the threshold.

SOMEONE TO LOOK UP TO:
A Lay View of Leadership

ISBN 978-0-6486684-0-4

Christian church leadership training tends to be taught by leaders, with little input from those being led. This book aims to fill in that gap. It explores the old days, Scriptural example, how to avoid spiritual abuse, and ideas for new ways forward.

Personal, disarming, and Biblically based, it aims to help leaders better understand those in their care, and to shape current and emerging ministries with compassion and forethought.

DAY IN THE SUN
Rebekah Robinson

Music CD

This pop/rock album contains ten songs to impart hope and inspire a deeper walk with Christ.

Available on iTunes and Spotify, and also in hard copy from the author at beck@beckoncreative.biz.

SOMEONE TO LOOK UP TO
STUDY NOTEBOOK

ISBN 978-0-6486684-1-1

A study guide and student workbook in one, this booklet is a companion volume for use in Bible college classrooms or study groups. It explores the principles of practical and theological leadership raised in *Someone to Look Up To*, encouraging reflection, prayer, and dialogue.

These five units prompt all the questions you were afraid to ask, and provide jotting space to delve into the issues.

www.ingramcontent.com/pod-product-compliance
Lightning Source LLC
Chambersburg PA
CBHW051450290426
44109CB00016B/1695